To Tim and Frances Armytage

. . . right as the herte of a man deliteth in
savour that is soote, right so the conseil of
trewe freendes yeveth swetnesse to the soule
Melib. 1157

CHAUCER

John Lawlor
**Professor of English Language and
Literature in the University of Keele**

HUTCHINSON UNIVERSITY LIBRARY
LONDON

HUTCHINSON & CO (*Publishers*) LTD

178–202 Great Portland Street, London W1

London Melbourne Sydney
Auckland Bombay Toronto
Johannesburg New York

First published 1968

*This book has been set in Fournier, printed in Great Britain
on Smooth Wove paper by Anchor Press, and
bound by Wm. Brendon, both of Tiptree, Essex*

09 088340 3 (cased)
09 088341 1 (paper)

CHAUCER

English Literature

Editor
JOHN LAWLOR
Professor of English Language and Literature
in the University of Keele

CONTENTS

Foreword   9

Introduction   11

1   Adventures of a Dreamer: 19
    The Book of the Duchess, The House of Fame,
    The Parliament of Fowls

2   The writer as dependant: 47
    Troilus and Criseyde (I)

3   *Tragedye* and tragedy: 70
    Troilus and Criseyde (II)

4   A return to authority: 90
    The Legend of Good Women

5   Tales and tellers: 105
    The Canterbury Tales (I)

6   *Auctoritee* and *pref:*   140
    The Canterbury Tales (II)

Notes   165

Selected Bibliography   177

Index   179

FOREWORD

This book is concerned with Chaucer as a narrative poet. Facts of his time including the dates of his principal works are easily come by elsewhere. The Selected Bibliography lists some of those works which a beginner will find most helpful.

I have suggested throughout that understanding of Chaucer must be based on steady recognition of the predominantly oral nature of his work, a poetry which normally has its first publication when it is read by the author to a small and courtly audience. The Introduction therefore sets out the principal respects in which poetry of this kind differs from that written for the eye of the solitary and general reader; and in each subsequent chapter time is spent on the characterisation of the narrator—the 'I' who reports either his own dream-adventures, or other men's experience as it can be found in 'olde bokes' or as he himself has heard it related—and on the variety of moves (especially the preliminary ones) by which the audience's attention is focused on the main matter in hand, however many (and delightful) the issues that are interwoven with it.

Since this book is designed for a relatively inexperienced reader there is no detailed treatment of narrative sources, intellectual history or modes of composition. But I have assumed on the reader's part an interest in the practical problems and varying solutions (not all of them successful) that occur in one highly original writer's career. With this in mind, I refer frequently to the tension between *auctoritee* and

---

auctoritee literally, authority; hence the written statement of an authority

experience (or *pref*) as the characteristically medieval form of a peren-
nially absorbing problem—the uncrossable differences between what
the writer must receive upon report and what he can truly know for
himself.

Given this interest, the reader will be in the best position to profit
from specialised treatments, a few of which are listed in the Selected
Bibliography; and he will be suitably guarded against uncritical
acceptance of those scholarly positions which, all unwittingly, substi-
tute dutiful and often laborious submission for direct contact.

The text used throughout is that of Robinson (2nd edn. 1957); and
throughout help is given to a reader unfamiliar with Chaucer's
language. I have not hesitated to repeat this information where
necessary; and I have even tried to tie down two classes of highly
deceptive words—those which, largely unchanged in form, are dis-
tinctly changed in meaning, and those which have lost an original
technical sense. On all occasions I have tried to supply a translation
for the particular context and not a generalised gloss. The proficient
reader is asked to bear with this. It seemed better to risk annoying him
than to allow the less experienced reader to be silently misled.

JOHN LAWLOR

---

pref proof, in the sense of that which is capable of being tested by experience

INTRODUCTION

Chaucer's high reputation has never been seriously in doubt: but it is a curious fact that the nature of his poetic achievement remains an open question. Mere primacy, of course, has much to answer for. Chaucer has long been a national institution, like the Abbey in which (though as royal servant, rather than poet) he lies buried. To each succeeding age he has been, indisputably, far off and long ago. The best of his admirers in an epoch of conscious refinement paid their tribute by rewriting what they took to be honest but unpolished productions: and a later age, valuing realistic fiction above all other literary achievement, was quick to seize upon *Troilus and Criseyde* and *The Canterbury Tales* as very early stages in the emergence of the novel. It happens that criticism of the present day shares the preoccupation of Chaucer's earliest admirers.[1] In the fifteenth and sixteenth centuries it was agreed that Chaucer was a master of poetic language—whether that language was seen as appropriate 'augmentation' of a needy vernacular, or as itself a 'well of English vndefyled', language in an imagined original purity. That kind of praise tells us much about the devotees; it tells us, too, something about the range of Chaucer's language that it should attract both kinds of praise; but it leaves us in the dark as to his real achievement, that 'character of an author which distinguishes him from all others and makes him appear that individual poet whom [we] would interpret'.[2] All this is matter for encouragement to anyone who comes to Chaucer for the first time. There is a universal chorus of praise, but no exact ground of assessment.

[1] Superior figures refer to Notes, pp. 165–75.

One of the contributors to a recent critical symposium takes as 'the most common denominator in Chaucer's literary personality a certain air of insouciance'. 'He seems', the critic continues, 'perpetually to be conducting a conversation with friends.' This, which clearly sets him apart from most other poets in our tradition, is no doubt attributable to his poetry being primarily oral in conception and delivery, on which more will be said presently. But what is to be noticed is that this sanctions inconsistency—'of tone, or of perspective, or of detail, as his narrative goes along'.[3] This is well said, warning us not only to be alert when we read Chaucer himself but correspondingly on our guard when his critics would offer us neat patterns of interpretation. 'Understandest thou what thou readest?' is a question that should awaken some reserve. Our first point, then, is to note in Chaucer a potential for surprising improvisation—to confront us on occasion with a sudden shift from gravity to overt fun; or, with more deliberation, to sustain a vein of humour which threatens to undercut the solemnity we might think appropriate. Another critic has reminded us that Arcite's dying is on a strange mixture of notes—

> His spirit chaunged hous and wente ther,
> As I cam nevere, I kan nat tellen wher—[4]   (A 2809–10)

and the late C. S. Lewis complained that in *The Book of the Duchess* a Knight who must insist on his dead lady's beauty in order to convince an obtuse Dreamer, 'makes the one seem a bore, and the other a fool, thus producing comic effects which are disastrous'.[5]

What, then, is to be done? It will not help much if we talk either about Chaucer's *naïveté*—implying that we must descend to him—or his 'mocking humour'—which places him above us in sophistication. There is no escape from an attentive and unprejudiced reading. If we can place ourselves among the circle of friends he is addressing, we shall be best positioned to follow his leading, whatever the surprises and apparent reversals of the journey, or dance, that follows. We may sympathise with those who have been disconcerted; for there will certainly be times when the mood we would think appropriate is not so much counterpointed as all but contradicted, most often by the poet inviting us to laugh. On these occasions it is as though he were playing the game 'O'Grady says', and trying very hard to catch us out.

Well, we must do our best to join in the game, and not mind too much
if sometimes we are found on the wrong foot. The poet's own standpoint is both solemn (as he speaks from his 'olde bokes') and
comic (since, poor man, he can do no other). He is therefore well
qualified to lead the game; and he must, right to the last syllable,
keep one move ahead. If the modern reader needs any consolation prize,
let him conjecture how many of Chaucer's original circle may have
given up in humorous despair. In what follows I list three main obstacles
to joining that circle—involuntary predispositions on the part of
the modern reader that limit or may altogether inhibit an unqualified
response. There is, happily, no master-key to the understanding of
Chaucer; but since claims in that direction have sometimes been
assumed (rather than explicitly made) I give under each head my
reasons for rejecting them.

The first characteristic that will strike the modern reader is Chaucer's
apparent digressiveness—the disproportions, as we conceive the
matter, between the tale proper and the whole extent of its telling.
If, for example, we take *The Book of the Duchess*, it appears that 444
lines are occupied with preliminaries—the love-suffering of the
narrator, followed by an unashamed re-telling of one of Ovid's stories,
then, in turn, a dream-experience, which leads by way of May morning,
the Romance of the Rose, a hunting-party, and, of all things, a puppy,
at last into the deep wood where we meet 'a man in blak', and our story
can begin. With this extended example of structural inconclusiveness
we may take a hundred lesser instances where the story is, as we would
think, held up by sententious observations on man, destiny, providence and free-will; diversified by reminders of the writer's illustrious
predecessors; or studded with allusions to comparable instances of
wisdom, beauty, cunning or malice—even if they are listed only to be
loftily dismissed as falling short of the matter in the hand. If there is
one quality which the characteristic Chaucerian narrative does *not*
have (the comic realism of the *fabliaux* always excepted) it is the
athletic, pace-making manner where effects are steadily cumulative,
so that ideally each line and verse-paragraph adds to episode or
characterisation. Against this, Chaucer is allusive, digressive, ready to
protest his inadequacy in comparison with his illustrious forbears,
but not very ready to get on with the story. Faced with this, the

modern reader is usually counselled to find out something about the medieval rhetoricians and to see in their precepts Chaucer's essential practice. It is sound general advice: but we should beware of regarding the rules of medieval rhetoric as constituting a code of practice to which the writer of necessity, and in meticulous detail, conforms. Indeed, as one writer has convincingly shown, 'Chaucer's use of certain "rhetorical" terms merely indicates a generalised knowledge rather than a technical acquaintance with it'.[6] The fact that much of Chaucer's knowledge of the art was indirect may encourage us to respect the freedom and variety of his practice. Some think that if *ars poetica* is a poor guide, *ars predicandi* may be better.[7] But what is prior to all this, and of first importance for the modern reader, is to re-examine in the light of these *artes* his own inherited conception of what literature *is*. Where books are few and are multiplied, if at all, at much expense, they are as far removed as possible from the ephemeral. We can expect a certain solidity of content—which means that useful matter will be looked for in any work that goes beyond the lightness of mere lyric. The 'story' itself is in no way original: it comes from common stock, and part of its essential charm is its familiarity. The task of the writer will be—with due deference to his great predecessors —to re-set the familiar material, and, with ordinary luck, to bring out new aspects of its universal truth. His art is therefore much less like that of the story-teller as we ordinarily think of him, and much more like that of the jeweller. The setting is intricate, highly wrought, and by no means merely a vehicle for the central gem. To enter into this imaginatively we must banish those conceptions of order and relevance which derive from an era of mass-multiplication of books by mechanical printing (so that our habitual expectation is one subject—one book). When we listen to Chaucer our aim must be to share a world in which books are the rarest of commodities. The 'profit' we can expect, along with the 'delight' proper to the story itself, is unashamedly sententious and is inseparable from the whole act of narration; and no one topic, faithfully pursued, is without reference to all others in the realm of knowledge—can the narrator but find the right *auctoritees* to help us on our way. It is against this background that 'rhetorical'

---

ars poetica the art of poetry (-making)   *ars predicandi* the art of preaching

devices naturally arise and pass from one writer to another in delighted imitation. Geoffrey de Vinsauf, the author of that vastly overrated handbook, *Poetria Nova*, wrote soundly of the natural aim of the writer, given this whole tradition:

> multiplice forma
> Dissimuletur idem; varius sis et tamen idem—[8]

that is, he must persist in saying the same thing differently. It is a counsel to which the medieval writer is naturally obedient. Everything in his environment predisposes him in that direction: there needs no Vinsauf come from the schoolroom to tell him this. More will be said about certain formal devices of rhetoric, when we come to examine particular poems. At the moment, the point to be emphasised is that we are not to strain to identify at every turn particular rhetorical devices. (It is, after all, the whole art of writing—even if in the weaker practitioners it becomes the art of fine writing.) Much more, the need is to accustom ourselves to a difference of standpoint. Instancing *The Book of the Duchess*, a few pages earlier, I mentioned the apparent disproportion of the preliminaries to the story. Can it now be suggested that things are rather the other way around? The 'story'—the exchanges between Knight and Dreamer—is part of the continuing dream-adventure rather than its appointed destination. What is essential to our understanding of the 'los' which finally confronts us is the whole situation of a narrator presented as an unsuccessful lover, who in his distress and near-despair meets one who claims to have experienced the heaven of fulfilled love. Nothing will alert us to the *capacity* of the Dreamer for receiving the Knight's story—and hence allow us to participate freely in the whole situation—unless we have first attuned ourselves to the characterisation Chaucer deftly establishes for him.

The second major consideration arises if we turn from the 'profit', or *lore*, expected by the audience to the 'delight', or *lust*, which should be inseparable from it. To do this is, in one sense, to turn from the solid ground of *auctoritee*, a world of entrenched if sometimes ambiguous counsel, to the dubious area of *pref*, what a man may in fact hope

---

multiplice forma etc. See that your constant theme appears in many different guises; be diverse, yet always the same   *los* loss   *lore* learning, knowledge *lust* pleasure

to encompass in his own experience. *Lust* commonly (though not exclusively) means, for a sophisticated audience, the unfailingly interesting matter of love. On this the poet can discourse at large; for there is absolutely no question that *he* can claim experience in these high matters. His place is the least in terms of *pref*; and he stands last in the long line of story-tellers. What then can he do but rehearse once more his *auctoritees*? It is a stance which corresponds with his own position in actuality, playing minstrel or *joculator* to those who honour him with their attention.[9] We may see in this the possibility of paradox. If love has its *auctoritees*, but the narrator at least (he will say nothing about his listeners) may not claim *pref*, actual experience of the high matters so confidently asserted by others, then we may come to suspect that *auctoritee* is the shadow and *pref* the substance. Some, at least, may be able to get on without *auctoritee*. One Canterbury pilgrim roundly says so:

> Experience, though noon auctoritee
> Were in this world, is right ynogh for me ...   (III 1–2)

and other persons, perhaps even a majority, can be seen to imply it by their actions. There is, then, an ample scope not merely for set-piece mock-heroic but for an irrepressible current of burlesque—a spring that, like the Mariner's brook, may sing a quiet tune but never stays underground for long. Yet this does not make only for humour. It means that *auctoritee*, what the books say, cannot be wholly a final Court of Appeal. Any quick resort to moral judgment is restrained by sympathy and, at least, silence, if the record offers nothing that can be said in extenuation.

In all this, we shall not be helped by confident references to 'Courtly Love', as a system of great clarity and consistency and marked above all by its rigorous opposition to the idea of marriage. The reader who would like to see how abstraction and determined simplification can create a scholarly myth will find E. T. Donaldson's treatment peculiarly instructive.[10] It only remains to add that the notion of 'Courtly Love' is firmly entrenched in a hundred textbooks and commentaries. Against all blandishments, the reader must attend to Chaucer. Let him repeat

---

joculator entertainer   *right ynogh* quite enough

to himself the simple truth that in the Knight's Tale Palamon and Arcite were both so misguided as to want to marry Emelye.

Shall we take Chaucer to task for knowing no better? If so, a third and final consideration arises. To insist on the plain sense of what Chaucer or his characters say, the 'text withouten nede of glose', we shall incur the wrath of another group of systematists. Starting from the proposition that all secular literature is to be understood in the same terms as scriptural and homiletic writing, the exegetes, who are most forcefully represented by D. W. Robertson and Bernard Huppé, make short work of the 'literal' or 'surface' meaning of any given work. Their concern is with the 'fruit' not the 'chaff', and they do not scruple to set Chaucer right where he himself is in error. As one reviewer wrote, much more in sorrow than in anger, to accept interpretation of this order 'we would have to assume that what Chaucer means . . . is almost the opposite of what he says'.[11] But that is no barrier to the determined exegete. Chaucer may make his 'retracciouns', renouncing tales that 'sownen into synne'. But Chaucer was wrong; they all 'sownen into' virtue, if we will only learn to read them aright.[12] If our older authors must be squeezed to provide the pabulum of an extraordinarily narrow education, it is perhaps as well that they do not confound their teachers by presenting themselves for examination. Yet even that might make no difference. Shakespeare's ghost, we remember, sat for a Civil Service post; and he did badly, having failed to read Bradley. Chaucer, if alive today, would have to study his Huppé.

All this is not to suggest that the reader will fare best if he dives in headlong, scorning any learned help. I have already suggested that a re-examination of preconceptions which equate literature with the printed book will be the best initial step. The next is readiness to hear the living voice from the page—to treat Chaucer's text as predominantly an oral script, allowing and sustaining such distinct opportunities for the oral narrator as mime, gesture, change of tone, dramatic pause, and significant reticence, the whole set in a small, courtly audience's genial acceptance of their own entertainer. Here is the setting for a perpetual 'conversation with friends', and here is the encouragement

---

glose explanation, commentary, hence (sometimes) special pleading, deceit
retracciouns retractions, withdrawals   *sownen into synne* conduce to sin

for an 'amiable inconsistency' and for 'artistic insouciance'.[13] The
fundamental framework of assumption (man's place in a patterned
universe which is the master-work of omnipotent and benevolent
Deity), together with leading instances of the *auctoritees* Chaucer loves
both to honour and on occasion to question—these can best be
encountered in that masterpiece of brief exposition, C. S. Lewis's
Discarded Image,[14] as a preparation for, and an illuminating accom-
paniment to, more extended works of exposition. But the real necessity
is to join the small audience, and listen to an artist who does not
inveigh or vaticinate—one who could not, even if he chose, speak
'within a circle of stage fire'.[15] Chaucer stays in the circle of a small and
familiar audience, whom he always treats with due deference, so that
the 'I' of his story-telling, with whatever variety of humorous and
even pathetic effect, remains one who learns by making mistakes, one
who by indirection finds direction out. Here is the fruitful opposition
for a writer between what we are solemnly assured is true (the *auctoritees* who encompass his tale) and the *pref*, won at the expense of the
'I' of the story, and sometimes in the teeth of his strongest initial
convictions. *The Book of the Duchess* is his first venture in this highly
individual art. It is time to join him.

I

ADVENTURES OF A DREAMER

The Book of the Duchess

The House of Fame

The Parliament of Fowls

Has any major poet opened his career with an undertaking more hazardous than Chaucer's? *The Book of the Duchess* is not, of course, his first attempt at poetry: but it is the first completed poem we have from his hand. It attempts consolation of the patron; as such it is expressive of duty and courtesy. But it eschews doctrinaire comfort, and is therefore marked by tenderness. It is 'a refusal to mourn'; but it faces loss with utter frankness. The poet, even in this hour of darkness, is still an entertainer, one who can only hope to make headway by diverting his patron, drawing a gleam of amusement for his own incomprehension. As such, the task calls for all the resources of maturity. That Chaucer at this earliest stage attempts it at all must be thought marvellous. What makes the attempt possible is less a matter of literary skill, marked as that is, than a delicacy of spirit—an unwillingness to intrude and an entire readiness to be set aside as uncomprehending—which is the epitome of perfect manners, *gentillesse*. If his training in the ways of a Court had done no more for him, Chaucer's offering for John of Gaunt, mourning the death of Blanche his Duchess, would remain one of the undoubted achievements of courtesy, a willing subordination of the self in face of the needs of another.

(I)

The modern reader must see Chaucer standing in the circle of a small society, each known to him, and each his feudal superior, as the

Corpus Christi MS 'frontispiece' shows him to us.[1] His task is hazardous indeed; his first problem therefore to open the range, to gain some distance from his audience. In this he differs most markedly from the author of a printed book, who meets an unknown audience through the silent traffic of the printed page; and who can meet that audience only as an individual, a solitary reader, in every instance. The traditional problem of the novelist has therefore been to gain intimacy, to establish and sustain a one-to-one relationship between himself and his 'gentle reader'. The task of the oral narrator is exactly the opposite. He must win a certain detachment (and resourcefully vary it, in tune with the developing needs of the story) away from his small, well-known audience, who are unalterably a group, with a group's reactions. His working principle is skilful opportunism, based upon a self-characterisation which springs from the literary tradition in which he works—last and therefore decidedly least of those who re-tell the stories adorned by their great predecessors—and from his actual position, the humble servant of those who are his social superiors.

Given this initial characterisation, the narrator can of course spring some surprises on his audience. He can gently deride, often by an exaggerated deference, their too-easy assumptions, and he can vary the tone from quiet humour to outright fun. The form which will above all others sanction a departure from actuality, cushion any shock of self-recognition, and finally allow the 'I' of the story to dissolve back into the familiar figure of the poet, is of course the dream-poem. In the three poems that follow, *The Book of the Duchess*, *The House of Fame*, and *The Parliament of Fowls*[2] Chaucer variously exploits the possibilities of a narrator who has to recount what passes his understanding. The skills he deploys are varied; his repertoire ranges from set-piece direct address to skilfully placed 'aside', and includes outright mimicry as well as adroitly timed question. But in each instance there is a common situation from which all else springs— the predicament of an 'I' who, in the end, must learn from his experience; and, seeing this, the audience begins to gain access to the story, to have it more nearly as a thing of their own possessing. A ruefully inadequate Dreamer has served his purpose when the reality he had ignored or minimised is plain for all to see. There is, then, no question of truths that come through, if they come at all, on the poet's terms.

The entire setting, social and intellectual, of Chaucer's art, precludes statements *ex cathedra*. What we hear from the *pulpitulum* is a confession of all-too-human weakness, that readiness to prejudge all things from the imagined safety of entrenched doctrine which is never so promptly called into play as when the woes are those of another.

(II)

Chaucer begins *The Book of the Duchess* by establishing two matters of immediate—but unstated—relevance to his present audience. The poet is deep in grief, deprived of sleep, and has

> felynge in nothyng,
> But, as yt were, a mased thyng.   (11–12)

Such a course, if persisted in, can have only one ending; and already his 'spirit of quyknesse' is dead (1–29). In this opening gambit Chaucer has challenged the grievous indifference to life of the mourning John of Gaunt. The sickness the poet feigns as his own preserves propriety, but the reference none the less comes home. It is immediately followed by a side-step away from the nature of present sorrow, arising from bereavement, into a veiled allusion, which courtly ears are quick to catch, to the cause of the poet's illness and its long duration:

> a sicknesse
> That I have suffred this eight yeer,
> And yet my boote is never the ner;
> For there is phisicien but oon
> That may me hele ...   (36–40)

No question now of the nature of the poet's sickness, nor of its hopeless quality. But this time sickness is a matter of delicate absurdity. The poet as hapless lover is an established role, and its humour is self-evident to the audience. Both the first move and the second perfectly exemplify the balance Chaucer is to hold throughout his poem. Sorrow is real, in the patron; in the poet it is touched with absurdity.

---

cathedra throne   *pulpitulum* reading-desk   *mased* dazed, bewildered
quyknesse life, vitality   *boote* cure   *hele* heal

Death is in the background; Love is now moved into the foreground.
One life is all but suspended—

> Alway in poynt to falle a-doun—

the other lingers on, sighing fruitlessly—

> Passe we over untill eft;
> That will not be mot nede be left   (41–2)

The silence of real suffering set against the volubility of a would-be
lover who is fortified by such simple maxims as these—this constitutes
the essential strategy of the poem. By line 44 we are launched on the
tale of love's old and unsuccessful campaigner; but the link with the
patron's real predicament is most adroitly placed. If grief allows no
rest it is better to read for diversion than to kill time:

> me thoughte it beter play
> Then play either at ches or tables.   (50–1)

This constitutes both an apology for and an invitation to join the
present 'play'. It reinforces the earlier warning that prolonged grief is
'agaynes kynde' (16). How appropriate, then, to turn to stories which
exemplify 'the law of kinde', stories which 'clerkes' and 'other poets'
have

> put in rime
> To rede, and for to be in minde,
> While men loved the lawe of kinde.   (54–6)

The tale of 'Seys' and 'Alcyone' is a tale of bereavement: but,
again, it keeps a proper distance and perhaps stirs the mourning one to
the beginning of a perspective on his grief, by telling of a wife's
sorrow for a dead husband. Here the longing to see again the lost one
is powerfully conveyed. We go down into the dark valley where
Morpheus dwells:

> Ther never yet grew corn ne gras,
> Ne tre, ne [nothing] that ought was,

---

in poynt to on the point of   *eft* later, another time   *mot* must
play recreation   *ches* chess   *tables* backgammon   *agaynes kynde* contrary
to nature   *that ought was* of any worth

> Beste, ne man, ne noght elles,
> Save there were a fewe welles
> Came rennynge fro the clyves adoun,
> That made a dedly slepynge soun.   (157–62)

As though this came too close to the real valley of the shadow, Chaucer moves to lighten the tone, and with a characteristically medieval freedom the balance swings in a moment to unashamed comedy. The messenger must blow his horn right in the sleeper's ear and shout at the top of his voice before Morpheus

> with hys oon yë
> Cast up, axed, 'Who clepeth ther?'   (184–5)

This cheerful realism prepares for the gentler directness of the dead husband's counsel to his wife:

> Awake! let be your sorwful lyf!
> For in your sorwe ther lyth no red.
> For, certes, swete, I nam but ded;
> Ye shul me never on lyve yse.   (202–5)

The story over, however it may be with his audience, the lovelorn poet at least takes a turn for the better. He begins to desire sleep—though at first only in the spirit of one joining in a joke:

> in my game I sayde anoon—
> And yet me lyst ryght evel to pleye—   (238–9)

The aside is all-important. There is no question of an invitation to forget grief: only, as before, the suggestion that one might respond to the narrator by taking part in his 'game'. The serious point is that one is surely not to die by simple neglect: rather than that, let us comically vow to Morpheus—or Juno, or anybody!—a feather bed and a luxuriously appointed bedroom. And, in a moment, the spell works. We are off, this time into a true dream, one of the poet's own,

---

clyves cliffs *dedly* death-like *soun* sound *yë* eye *cast up* cocked open
axed asked *clepeth* calls *lyth no red* there is no profit *I nam but ded* lit.,
I am not other than dead; i.e. I am, in all truth, dead *on lyve* alive *yse* see
in my game in fun *anoon* presently *me lyst ryght evel to pleye* I didn't at
all feel like joking

                        a sweven
            So wonderful, that never yit
            Y trowe no man had the wyt
            To konne wel my sweven rede.   (276–80)

The poem has run for 290 of its 1334 lines, and we are still only on
the threshold of a meeting between the Dreamer and a sorrowing
Knight who tells us plainly that his lady is taken from him by Death.
But Chaucer has gone most skilfully to work. He has established that
long continuance in grief is against Nature: and that the dead, were
they to return, would counsel acceptance. Nature's remedy is sleep,
and innocent recreation. Let the patron enact this, by sharing in the
story of a dream, and attending to the hapless adventures of a rueful
lover, one who knows love only as unfulfilled desire, and for whose
suffering, gently tinged with ridicule as it is, no end is foreseeable.

    In the dream that follows, love itself is evoked in its first freshness—
love as perfected harmony, the pursuit of men from immemorial
times, the happiness especially appropriate to May Morning, birdsong,
story-telling, and unclouded skies (291–343). The theme is pursuit,
with the hope of attaining the highest earthly good. The hunt is up,
and all goes busily until the hart

                    rused, and staal away
            Fro alle the houndes a privy way.   (381–2)

Suddenly, all stands still:

                the hunte wonder faste
            Blew a forloyn at the laste.   (385–6)

The Dreamer follows a puppy, down a flower-strewn path into the
deeps of the forest; and amid many wonders of Nature he finds at
last a disconsolate human figure:

                    a man in blak,
            That sat and had yturned his bak
            To an ook, an huge tree.   (445–7)

---

sweven dream   *Y trowe* I'm sure   *wyt* intelligence, wisdom   *konne* know
how, be able   *rede* interpret   *rused* changed course   *staal* stole
hunte huntsman   *wonder faste* very quickly   *forloyn* recall   *ook* oak

The dress and the posture prompt only one reaction:

> 'Lord', thoght I, 'who may that be?
> What ayleth hym to sitten her?'   (448–9)

The appeal to Nature with which the poem had opened is powerfully reinforced by the setting of natural growth: and the lesson to turn from the fruitless past is brought home in the transition from winter to spring, to a place which

>   had forgete the povertee
> That wynter, thorgh hys colde morwes,
> Had mad hyt suffre, and his sorwes.
> All was forgeten, and that was sene,
> For al the woode was waxen grene.   (410–14)

It is against this background—the perennial contrast of spring and winter, natural growth in the present, as against fixed absorption in the past—that Chaucer conducts a dialogue between one who has experienced the reality of loss by death and one who (a suitable part for the courtly poet, in his entire dependence on books) knows love only as unfulfilled desire. This debate is pursued with great kindliness by the Dreamer, and is designed to draw out the Knight. But as it grows in intensity, the roles of voluble Dreamer and taciturn, inconsolable Knight begin to be reversed. It is the Knight who waxes eloquent in recalling the heaven of fulfilled love—a spring time, indeed—and the Dreamer who, in the end, forgetting alike all doctrinaire considerations and the fact he had learned at the outset, that the Lady is dead, can only ask

'Where is she now?'

At once, and for the last time, the hart-hunting is over: the 'forloyn' is heard again in the one syllable the Knight speaks, frozen into recollection:

> 'Now?' quod he, and stynte anoon.
> Therwith he wax as deed as stoon.   (1298–1300)

---

what ayleth hym? what is the matter with him?   *forgete* forgotten
morwes mornings   *his sorwes* winter's hardships   *sene* manifest   *waxen* grown
stynte stopped   *anoon* at once   *wax* grew, became   *stoon* stone

The Dreamer, as I have suggested elsewhere,[3] had hoped to bring consolation by pressing a question of the greater or less in loss. Which is the more grievous—loss by death, or loss by inconstancy? The theoretical question, debated in twin poems by the French poet Machaut, is well suited to one who, at the outset, had put on the traditional garb of innocence—one who knows all about love from his *auctoritees*, nothing about it by *pref*, for no Lady has ever yielded to him. Chaucer's achievement is in the perfect capitulation of this Dreamer as the love now brought to judgment is finally seen to transcend all imaginary instances. Only then, and unswervingly, can the audience be reminded of the reality of loss, a reality which has nothing to do with considerations of more or less.

The poem will work best for a reader who, like the Dreamer, actually forgets the plain truth he has heard at the start of the dialogue. But whether the reader can do this or not, he, like every member of Chaucer's audience before him, including the mourning John of Gaunt, must taste the sharpness of actuality before the poem ends. Pity does not, in the end, sanction any disguise. When a recollected heaven has done its work, then the hell of the present comes nakedly into view. For now, for the first time, it can be faced.

(III)

In *The House of Fame* the pace is, at first, leisurely. Dreams are curious things. Let us consider the kinds of dream; why do some dreamers differ in their experience from others?; is it all explicable in physiological terms?; and so on. The questions are raised, only to show that the whole subject is finally mysterious, and as such the subject of continuing debate:

> Wel worthe, of this thyng, grete clerkys,
> That trete of this and other werkes.   (53–4)

It all helps to establish the simplicity of the Dreamer—

> For I of noon opinion
> Nyl as now make mensyon—   (55–6)

Wel worthe, of this thyng, grete clerkys Good luck to profound scholars with this matter [with the implication, they'll need it]   *Nyl = ne + yl*   not

so that we can turn an unprejudiced eye on *his* dream: and the poet helps to lull us into this frame of mind by the simple patter of his 'Invocation', a sort of night-spell:

> whoso thorgh presumpcion,
> Or hate, or skorn, or thorgh envye,
> Dispit, or jape, or vilanye,
> Mysdeme hyt, pray I Jesus God
> That (dreme he barefot, dreme he shod),
> That every harm that any man
> Hath had, syth the world began,
> Befalle hym therof, or he sterve,
> And graunte he mote hit ful deserve ... (94-101)

Our defences are down: and it seems as well, for the story which follows is about as unsurprising as could be imagined—a dutiful re-telling of the story of Aeneas, with a suitable sprinkling of exclamatory utterance—

> 'But wel-away! the harm, the routhe,
> That hath betyd for such untrouthe!'— (383-4)

and a steady pushing-on of the successive episodes with 'Ther saugh I . . .', 'And also sawgh I . . .'. It is a relief to emerge with the Dreamer into the open air: here is at least the promise of something new:

> now wol I goo out and see,
> Ryght at the wiket, yf y kan
> See owhere any stiryng man
> That may me telle where I am. (476-9)

Neither the Dreamer nor, in fact, Geoffrey Chaucer could know it. But this adventurous step was to take Chaucer on a wide détour from the approved path for a courtly poet, the obedient servant of the God of Love whose true devotion shines in the laboured heroics of this first book—above all, in the chiding of male offenders against constancy—

---

thorgh through *Dispit* spite *jape* levity *vilanye* ill-breeding, unseemly conduct *Mysdeme* misconstrue [with the implication, wilfully] *or* before *sterve* die *routhe* pitiful condition *betyd* befallen, come about *untrouthe* infidelity, inconstancy *wiket* wicket (gate) *owhere* anywhere *stiryng* stirring, moving about

Loo, Demophon, duk of Athenys,
How he forswor hym ful falsly,
And traysed Phillis wikkidly ...   (388–90)

Eke lo! how fals and reccheles
Was to Breseyda Achilles,
And Paris to Oenone;
And Jason to Isiphile,
And eft Jason to Medea;
And Ercules to Dyanira,
For he left hir for Yole,
That made hym cache his deth, parde.
How fals eke was he Theseus,
That, as the story telleth us,
How he betrayed Adriane;
The devel be hys soules bane! ...   (397–408)

It is in fact to this strait path, the catalogue of villainous male offences
against Cupid's saints, that Chaucer is to be recalled, some years
later, by an outraged God of Love, incensed by his daring to tell of
female inconstancy.[4] But for the moment, the poet is off the chain.
The coast is clear—frighteningly so:

When I out at the dores cam,
I faste aboute me beheld,
Then sawgh I but a large feld,
As fer as that I myghte see,
Withouten toun, or hous, or tree,
Or bush, or grass, or eryd lond ...   (480–5)

In this trackless waste, without landmark of any sort, the poet must
ask to be saved

Fro fantome and illusion.   (493)

No sooner said, than done. Help is at hand: a friendly animal descends;
and with his descent one whole order of poetry is transformed.

If we wished to construct a standard recipe for a medieval courtly
poem, it might run:

---

traysed betrayed   *he Theseus* that Theseus   *bane* destruction   *faste* eagerly
eryd ploughed   *fantome* delusion

First, catch your bookish poet, a hopeless devotee of Love; the best specimens are to be found languishing on any fine May morning. Take from stock equal portions of encyclopaedic learning and familiar story. Season with cheerful irrelevance, garnish with rhetorical flourishes, and serve with becoming modesty.

Nothing is more instructive than the ease with which Chaucer, from the advent of the Eagle at the end of Book I, meets each of these demands. The poet is a servant of Love, yes: and the Eagle is properly condescending towards his innocence-by-*auctoritee*. The poet is modest? Certainly, and, as the Eagle triumphantly demonstrates, he has much to be modest about: the detail of a reverberant universe has to be expounded as well as encountered. Again, it is not to be disputed that a poet is a dependant; one who draws all, 'lust' and 'lore' alike, from his revered books. But was the point ever put so clearly, when we see this particular poet borne aloft, playing Baby to his grotesque Bird, reduced to monosyllables as stupefied listener and terror-stricken passenger? Of all the Eagle's traits, it is his self-absorption that gives the crowning touch. We see that the passenger must be content to accept the Eagle's learning, when it comes to the disposition of the stars, and not put matters to the test—because, as he says,

> they shynen here so bryghte
> Hyt shulde shenden al my syghte
> To loke on hem.   (1015–17)

It is a point which the Eagle had overlooked; but it does not detain him, beyond laconic acknowledgment:

> 'That may wel be',
> Quod he.   (1017–18)

The poet's incapacity for real experience, that characteristic standpoint of the courtly narrator, has never been more humorously conveyed than in this wondrous transformation of a Friendly Animal—the approved guide, in courtly poetry, to cover the hiatus from 'awaking' in the dream to the first steps in the dream-adventure. Friendly animals, very suitably, should have some marks of docility: Chaucer

---

shenden ruin

had turned Machaut's lion in *The Book of the Duchess* into a puppy, fawning endearingly at his feet. Now he soars up the scale. There is precedent again: Dante's wheeling Eagle, *terribil come folgor*, comes to mind. But, as always, Chaucer's own touch is evident. The first impression had been awe-inspiring—as if

> the heven had ywonne
> Al newe of gold another sonne—   (505–6)

while the second was plainly terrifying:

> with hys grymme pawes stronge,
> Withyn hys sharpe nayles longe,
> Me, fleynge, in a swap he hente.   (541–3)

But the Eagle turns out to be kindly; and with the announcement of his mission, condescension towards the passenger becomes comically insistent loquacity. The bookish servant of love is a figure of fun:

> [thou] peynest the to preyse hys art,
> Although thou haddest never part . . .   (627–8)

Yet bookish service will have an appropriate reward. The writer is no observer of the reality around him:

> Of thy verray neyghebores,
> That duellen almost at thy dores,
> Thou herist neyther that ne this.   (649–51)

He turns simply from one kind of book to another:

> For when thy labour doon al ys,
> And hast mad alle thy rekenynges,[5]
> In stede of reste and newe thynges,
> Thou goost hom to thy hous anoon;
> And, also domb as any stoon,
> Thou sittest at another book
> Tyl fully daswed ys thy look . . .   (652–8)

---

terribil come folgor fearful as the lightning (*Purg.* ix 29)   *ywonne* gained
Al newe wholly new   *pawes* talons   *in a swap* in one swoop   *hente* seized
peynest the take pains, toil away   *herist* hear   *rekenynges* accounts
newe thynges recreation   *anoon* right away   *domb* dumb   *daswed* dazed
(i.e. his eyes begin to swim)

It is against this background of impenetrable insulation that the Eagle offers the supreme prize, a gift of gracious Jove. The mere writer will be taken to that place where all that is spoken by lovers (all the true copy for a writer, hitherto dependent on written records) still resides—the 'kyndely stede', or gravitational centre, of all that once sounded from mortal lips. The theme is the Writer Liberated; and the freedom and energy of Book II mark a new dimension in Chaucer's writing. The comedy of the situation, a genial parody of that vein of didactic literature in which a disconsolate human figure is instructed by a heavenly visitant,[6] is sustained by the poet's accurate ear for self-delighting orotundity:

> Telle me this now feythfully,
> Have y not preved thus symply,
> Withoute any subtilite
> Of speche, or gret prolixite
> Of termes of philosophie,
> Of figures of poetrie,
> Or colours of rethorike—

which concludes with the complacent bathos

> Pardee, hit oughte the to lyke!   (853–60)

It calls for high versatility in the narrator, who must play both loquacious Eagle and timorous pupil. Book II is a dream of delight: what else had the poet to learn?

The answer is plain in Book III—the art of construction, or how to take your story to a conclusion. Once the Dreamer is on his own, invention begins to falter, and we are back at the bad old manner of dutiful categorisation: 'Tho sawgh I', 'Thoo gan I', 'Ther herde I', relieved by routine *occupatio* ('What shuld I make lenger tale?', 'Loo! how shulde I now telle al thys?'), and interspersed with mechanical *exclamatio* ('But, Lord! the perry and the richesse!').[7] Predictably, Chaucer turns to clowning. The great masters of story-telling are

---

ky ndely stede place appointed by Nature   *feythfully* honestly   *figures* ornamental devices   *colours* figures of speech   *Pardee!* my word!   *lyke* please   *occupatio* a refusal to describe (with the object of heightening the effect)   *exclamatio* apostrophe and/or exclamation (of wonder, grief, etc.)

seen in the pillared hall, and when it comes to the Trojan story something very like an uneasy human pyramid is uppermost in mind:

> Ful wonder hy on a piler
> Of yren, he, the gret Omer;
> And with him Dares and Tytus
> Before, and eke he Lollius,
> And Guydo eke de Columpnis,
> And Englyssh Gaufride eke, ywis;
> And ech of these, as have I joye,
> Was besy for to bere up Troye.
> So hevy therof was the fame
> That for to bere hyt was no game.   (1465–74)

We can see the tottering figure at the bottom of this insecure structure.
This is comic relief, indeed; but where is the main design? Chaucer
can find no alternative but the yeoman-work of painstaking description:

> this halle, of which I rede,
> Was woxen on highte, length, and brede,
> Wel more, be a thousand del,
> Than hyt was erst, that saugh I wel.   (1493–5)

Certainly, he does his best: and the procession of those who come to
seek favour at Fame's throne is conscientiously marshalled—eight
'companyes' of them, followed by a dervish-dance of those who
proclaim themselves

> shrewes, every wyght,
> And han delyt in wikkednesse,
> As goode folk han in godnesse.   (1830–2)

But not even the intervention of a friendly stranger (1869–71) will
serve. Blandly, the stranger assumes that the Dreamer is yet another
petitioner: and there is one more opportunity for comedy as the

---

yren iron (the metal appropriate to Mars, hence to those who write of war)
Omer Homer   *Dares, Tytus, Lollius, Guydo . . . de Columpnis, Gaufride* all
writers on the Trojan War, of whom *Lollius* is a dubious figure and *Gaufride*
Geoffrey of Monmouth   *no game* no light matter   *rede* speak   *brede* breadth
a thousand del a thousandfold   *erst* before   *shrewes* rascals

ow not even the advent of another authoritative figure can rescue us
nter

A man of gret auctorite . . .

ut the poem ends.

Why? It is disappointing after the verve of Book II; but on the
vidence of *The House of Fame* taken as a whole it seems that Chaucer
either rises to his topic with exhilaration or he clowns his way aim-
lessly forward. Something, of course, is attributable to the kind of
story he has chosen—the science-fiction of aerial voyaging to the
remote parts of the universe. It is the appropriate setting for a parody
of consolatory didacticism, and it allows an admirable pace and
sense of excitement. But, given the first fine flourishes of a promised
marvel, its realisation must always fall a little flat. 'What went ye out
for to see?' is inevitably a depressing question. The point, however,
goes deeper. Chaucer, it seems, triumphs when he can find an opportunity of inverting roles, of becoming, unexpectedly, the patient and
not the agent of his design. Anything less suits him not at all: he has,
in these terms, no middle range. We are back to the manner of Book I,
conscientious recital diversified by an occasional return of briskness
and relieved by outright humour.

It is early in his career to judge: but so far, at least, it seems that
Chaucer is a writer who is easily bored, so long as he is called upon to
conduct the narrative in his own person. But give him the opportunity
to become totally the patient of his story—to undergo its development,
powerless to intervene—and freedom of inventiveness, an irrepressible
energy, are at once in play. How much of this, one wonders, is attributable to his role as narrator in the presence of a small, known audience,
whose polite inattentiveness he might fear more than any evident
disapproval? The oral narrator's constant task is also his hardest—to
stir and to mould audience-reaction. The worst obstacle is not hostility,
but indifference. The oral narrator must have an audience he can play
to: and in such reversals as those the Dreamer encounters in *The House
of Fame* he can create one—himself the victim, playing straight man
to the magisterial interlocutor. The literary personality this brings
into focus is of course not peculiar to medieval settings. One thinks of

Dreamer's protest overflows on him. The positions o
pupil are momentarily reversed:

> '. . . these be no suche tydynges
> As I mene of.' 'Noo?' quod he.
> And I answered, 'Noo, parde!' (1894–6

But it is a momentary victory. Characteristically, the j
Dreamer; his interlocutor has neither understood nor cai

> 'Whych than be, loo, these tydynges
> That thou now [thus] hider brynges,
> *That thou hast herd?*' quod he to me;
> 'But now no fors, for wel y se
> What thou desirest for to here . . .' (1907–11)

Defeated, the Dreamer is driven back to his recital: an
return of the Eagle cannot mend matters. For now he talk
sober and uncharacteristic fashion. What was genially avu
become cloudily oracular:

> Syth that Fortune hath mad amys
> The [fruit] of al thyn hertys reste
> Languisshe and eke in poynt to breste . . . (2016–18)

What is to come of it all? The clamour begins to rise, and th
swells—

>   shipmen and pilgrimes,
> With scrippes bret-ful of lesinges,
> Entremedled with tydynges,
> And eek allone be hemselve.
> O, many a thousand tymes twelve
> Saugh I eke of these pardoners,
> Currours, and eke messagers,
> With boystes crammed ful of lyes . . . (2122–9)

---

no fors no matter *The [fruit] of al thyn hertys reste* the outcome which
would bring you entire heartsease *Languisshe* decline, wither *in poynt to*
breste ready to burst open *shipmen* seafarers *scrippes* wallets *bret-ful*
brimful *lesinges* lies *Entremedled* intermingled *hemselve* themselves
Currours couriers *boystes* boxes

B

Thackeray, pushing on with the story, impatient of his characters, even irritable at their shortcomings, diversifying his tales with ironic humour and sometimes discordantly high spirits, as though to assert his independence. The parallel is incomplete; Chaucer's compassion for his characters, as we shall see, is unfailing even to the point of embarrassed evasion when the whole truth would bear too hard on them. But contempt is a well-recognised defensive reaction; and when we find Thackeray achieving a unique point of vantage as the Showman of *Vanity Fair*, dispensed, as it were, from responsibility for the story, the parallel will hold so far. Chaucer is never so free as when the Dreamer is the puppet-like figure imprisoned in the Eagle's 'clawes starke'. There is a kind of literary genius or *daimon* which can only work with maximum effectiveness when the problem of auctorial personality is not so much solved, by adroit characterisation, as cancelled, by outright subordination. The author who can in this sense lose himself will assuredly find his highest creative power. Equally, whenever he cannot do so, a restless energy, a tendency to move to and fro on the margin of his story, or to interrupt its progress by a clowning which has more the marks of impatient diversion than genuine high spirits—these will be the signs of his inability to be absorbed in the telling. So far as Chaucer is concerned, it leads, as often as not, to the work remaining unfinished. *The Book of the Duchess* was saved by its external and overriding purpose, and its conclusion came with tactful haste, the world reassembling itself under comfortingly ordinary shapes as the clock struck to banish past time. In the absence of so compelling a purpose, the problem of ending the work may be insoluble. No 'man of gret auctorite', however impeccable his credentials, can save the story in which an author of this bent and susceptibility has failed to lose himself.

(IV)

In *The Parliament of Fowls*, at all events, there is no problem, in these terms, of identity. The poet is the bookish servant of Love, and his service is perfectly appropriate to a happy day. So far from disqualifying him, his dependence upon the *auctoritees* has a special suitability to this occasion of new beginnings:

> For out of olde feldes, as men seyth,
> Cometh al this newe corn from yer to yere,
> And out of olde bokes, in good feyth,
> Cometh al this newe science that men lere.   (22–5)

Consequently, there is, this time, no pressure of impending events. The Dreamer is not carried along on a tide of debate or insistent instruction. He tells of the book he has been reading; and it, in its turn, elaborates the role of dependant, in a double aspect—man as heir to ancestral wisdom, and mortal man as undergoing a brief alienation from his immortality:

> oure present worldes lyves space
> Nis but a maner deth.   (53–4)

The dream, this time, is an *Oraculum*.[8] Africanus appears to his descendant, and his purpose is to show the full setting of each human life in a universe that is itself in cyclic motion, moving back to its true point of origin and in doing so making mortal history ultimately insignificant:

> Thanne tolde he hym, in certeyn yeres space
> That every sterre shulde come into his place
> Ther it was first, and al shulde out of mynde
> That in this world is don of al mankynde.   (67–70)

Who but the bookish poet could suitably re-state this august theme? It is neatly given its special application to the matter of love. The universal law is one of harmonious interrelationship: those who specially offend against it are 'likerous folk'. Yet even for them, in the workings of benevolent providence, there is final forgiveness:

> But brekers of the lawe, soth to seyne,
> And likerous folk, after that they ben dede,
> Shul whirle aboute th'erthe alwey in peyne,
> Tyl many a world be passed, out of drede,
> And than, foryeven al hir wikked dede,
> Than shul they come into this blysful place ...   (78–83)

---

science knowledge   *lere* learn   *worldes* worldly, mortal   *Nis but a maner deth* is nothing but a kind of death   *sterre* star, heavenly body   *shulde out* would [pass] out   *likerous* lecherous   *soth to seyne* assuredly   *whirle aboute th'erthe* be tossed to and fro on earth   *many a world* many ages   *out of drede* without doubt, make no mistake

The solemn theme enunciated, Chaucer moves swiftly to lighten the
mood. He, too, falls asleep: could there be any connection between
the story he has been reading and the coming of Africanus to his own
bedside? 'Can I not seyn....' But Africanus can, and he is suitably
affable towards a dutiful student of battered volumes:

> Thow hast the so wel born
> In lokynge of myn olde bok totorn,
> Of which Macrobye roughte nat a lyte,
> That sumdel of thy labour wolde I quyte. (109–12)

The humour continues, in the Dreamer's brief invocation to Cytherea;
let her keep him straight—

> As wisly as I sey the north-north-west,
> Whan I began my sweven for to write— (117–18)

and it is characteristic that, as on a previous occasion, he has to be
seized bodily and taken on the next step in his adventure:

> This forseyde Affrican me hente anon ... (120)

But this hesitation serves its purpose. There is good reason to halt
before gates which proclaim an irrevocable choice. A timorous Dreamer
is evidence of the power of equal and opposite forces:

> Right as, betwixen adamauntes two
> Of evene myght, a pece of yren set
> Ne hath no myght to meve to ne fro—
> For what that oon may hale, that other let—
> Ferde I, that nyste whether me was bet
> To entre or leve ...   (148–53)

The moment of poise dissolves into comedy—

> Affrycan, my gide,
> Me hente, and shof in at the gates wide. (153–4)

---

totorn tattered   *Macrobye* Macrobius, author of the major commentary on
Scipio's Dream   *roughte nat a lyte* cared a lot   *sumdel* somewhat   *quyte*
requite   *wisly* surely   *sey the* saw thee (the planet Venus)   *sweven* dream
hente seized   *anon* immediately, without more ado   *adamauntes* loadstones
evene myght equal strength   *meve* move   *hale* attract   *let* hinders, repels
Ferde I I fared   *nyste* = *ne*+*wyste* did not know   *shof* shoved

For now the incapacity of a bookish servant of Love guarantees his immunity from punishment—or perfected happiness. The standard gibe comes with its familiar application:

> But natheles, although that thow be dul,
> Yit that thow canst not do, yit mayst thow se... (162–3)

As before, in *The House of Fame*, the writer will be rewarded by first-hand acquaintance with appropriate material:

> if thow haddest connyng for t'endite,
> I shal the shewe mater of to wryte.   (167–8)

But this time there is a gentler conclusion:

> With that myn hand in his he tok anon,
> Of which I confort caughte, and wente in faste.   (169–70)

It is a suitable transition, for now the Dreamer begins to recede as a character. His adventure, as such, is over: henceforward, what we are to be shown in the poem we shall see for ourselves. There is no further place for sustained comedy at the expense of a bumbling Dreamer, learning only by the hard knocks of experience and rescued, if at all, by the final intervention of any 'man of gret auctorite'. From line 171 onwards the poet concentrates on the region of fulfilled happiness, a land of eternal spring, unshadowed by age or sickness:

> No man may there waxe sek ne old
>   ... ne nevere wolde it nyghte,
> But ay cler day to any manes syghte.   (207, 209–10)

All the persons sacrosanct to Love are to be found here; and presiding over all, and fairest of all, is Nature:

> ther sat a queene
> That, as of lyght the somer sonne shene
> Passeth the sterre, right so over mesure
> She fayrer was than any creature.   (298–301)

---

connyng for t'endite literary ability   *waxe* grow   *sek* sick   *ay* ever,
perpetually   *shene* bright, radiant   *Passeth* surpasses   *sterre* star   *over*
mesure beyond (all) reckoning

The tapestried review of Love and Love's servants, including the portrait of Venus herself—

> Hyre gilte heres with a golden thred
> Ibounden were, untressed as she lay,
> And naked from the brest unto the hed
> Men myghte hire sen—   (267–70)

leads up to the final focus upon 'this noble goddesse Nature', enthroned upon 'seynt Valentynes day'

> Whan every foul cometh there to chese his make.   (310)

At once, stillness gives way to noise; the procession of single figures as the poet's eye has fallen on them, one by one, dissolves into a wide and crowded canvas—

> So huge a noyse gan they make
> That erthe, and eyr, and tre, and every lake
> So ful was, that unethe was there space
> For me to stonde, so ful was al the place.   (312–15)

For a moment the Dreamer is brought into close-up; and it is appropriate that he should, so to speak, counter with a learned reference. Alanus's *De Planctu Naturae* reminds us not only of Nature's sovereignty but also of that hierarchical system derived from her sovereignty which now allows the writer to establish order in the crowded scene.[9] From line 323 ('That is to seyn . . .', a characteristic turn) to line 364, we see the order of the assembly, from 'foules of ravyne' who are 'hyest set', down to

> The throstil old; the frosty feldefare.

---

gilte golden   *untressed* unbraided   *chese* choose   *make* mate, spouse
eyr air   *unethe* scarcely   *De Planctu Naturae* 'The Complaint of Nature', by
Alanus de Insulis (*c.* 1128–1203), a mixture of prose and verse (in this
resembling Boethius and Martianus Capella) in which Nature complains that
man alone is disobedient to her rule of law   *foules of ravyne* birds of prey
The throstil old; the frosty feldefare the long-lived thrush and that bird of
winter, the fieldfare

'What shulde I seyn?': they are all there, and each has only one purpose—under Nature's presidency

> Benygnely to chese or for to take,
> By hire acord, his formel or his make.   (370–1)

Chaucer ends his survey, our last reminder of the observer, abruptly. 'But to the poynt', he says (372), and we are off, to attend to the proceedings without distraction.

Things turn out rather differently from anything these ordered preliminaries may have led us to expect. Nature holds

> A formel egle, of shap the gentilleste
> That evere she among hire werkes fond,   (373–4)

and it is soon apparent that, whatever happens to lesser creatures in their choice of partners, the most aristocratic birds, the 'tersel' eagles, are vying with each other for her favours. The grounds on which the successive claims are put forward are progressively complex. All the medieval love of debate is here, not only in the arguments of mounting complexity concerning free choice but also in the sense that there must be a predestined election—if only it can be traced out. The preliminaries will have done their work if we hear these subtle pleas against a background of ultimate order and harmony, the constituent principle of the Universe, personified in Nature herself—

> the vicaire of the almyghty Lord,
> That hot, cold, hevy, lyght, moyst, and dreye
> Hath knyt by evene noumbres of acord.   (379–81)

The foreground is one of forensic subtlety. But even the most cogent of pleas must be directed towards the free choice of the lady. Agreement must be 'By hire acord'; and in the play upon 'acord' we have centrally affirmed the principle of harmony upon which all turns, on earth as in heaven.

The first claimant takes the high and apparently unassailable ground of absolute submission to the Lady's 'mercy'. His plea is for pity on

---

Benygnely graciously   *chese* choose   *acord* agreement   *formel* female eagle
or hawk   *tersel* tercel, the male in any species of hawk   *vicaire* deputy
dreye dry   *knyt* joined   *acord* harmony, agreement

his woeful state: 'merci', 'grace', 'routhe' are all any suitor can ask, but they are surely enough:

> Thanne oughte she be myn thourgh hire mercy,
> For other bond can I non on hire knette. (437–8)

But complication follows, in the speech of another 'tersel egle', one 'Of lower kynde':

> I love hire bet than ye don, by seint John,
> Or at the leste I love hire as wel as ye,
> And lenger have served hire in my degre... (451–3)

If duration, the length of a love-sickness, is a prime test of its genuineness and therefore the more urgent claim upon 'mercy'—an immediate ending of sorrow too long endured—then the conclusion is obvious:

> if she shulde have loved for long lovynge,
> To me ful-longe hadde be the guerdonynge. (454–5)

This, like the first plea, is apparently unanswerable. But a third 'tersel' has yet another case, this time adroitly introduced by a reminder that time must have a stop—

> Now, sires, ye seen the litel leyser heere;
> For every foul cryeth out to ben ago
> Forth with his make, or with his lady deere. (464–6)

Sweetheart ('make') or lady, it is all one, he claims; the reality is passion, and the important consideration is not duration, but intensity:

> Of long servyse avaunte I me nothing;
> But as possible is me to deye to-day
> For wo as he that hath ben languysshyng
> This twenty wynter, and wel happen may,
> A man may serven bet and more to pay
> In half a yer, although it were no moore,
> Than som man doth that hath served ful yoore. (470–6)

---

routhe pity *knette* fasten *ful-longe* long since [the alternative reading, *allone* (alone) is perhaps preferable] *hadde be* would have been *guerdonynge* reward (the lady's favour) *leyser* leisure, rest *ago* gone *bet* better *more to pay* give greater pleasure *ful yoore* for a long time

It is, perhaps, an application of the parable 'Unto this last' (Matt. xx, 14). Certainly, it exposes the difficulty of a merely distributive justice (the best reward to the best claimant); and it is the beginning of long debate:

> from the morwe gan this speche laste
> Tyl dounward drow the sonne wonder faste.   (489–90)

It looks as though this St Valentine's Day is going to end without a single match-making, let alone a universal pairing, from the 'tercels' down to the lowest ranks. The clamour rises: aristocratic finesse in debate is all very well in its place, but not now:

> 'Com of!', they cried, 'allas, ye wol us shende!
> Whan shal youre cursede pletynge have an ende?'   (494–5)

Refinements of theory can be tolerated, up to a point: but when practical satisfaction is in question, then we hear the realist, putting the case for *pref* as unanswerable:

> How sholde a juge eyther parti leve
> For ye or nay, withouten any preve?   (496–7)

The same note is heard, but raucously, when the duck, a true plebeian, derides the turtle-dove, that genteel admirer of aristocratic ways. The 'turtle trewe' had rebuked 'the fol kokkow' for taking it upon himself to speak for 'worm-foul'—'office uncommytted ofte anoyeth' (518), she says tartly. When her turn comes, as duly elected representative of the 'sed-foul', she shows herself delicately besotted with high sentiment:

> 'Nay, God forbede a lovere shulde chaunge!'
> The turtle seyde, and wex for shame al red,
> 'Though that his lady everemore be straunge,
> Yit lat hym serve hire ever, til he be ded ...'   (582–5)

---

drow drew, sank   *Com of!* come on!   *shende* ruin   *pletynge* argument
preve proof   *turtle* turtle-dove   *fol kokkow* foolish cuckoo   *office uncommytted
ofte anoyeth* taking it upon yourself to speak for others often leads to trouble
wex ... al red blushed deeply   *straunge* distant

To this starry-eyed idealism common sense knows only one reply:

> 'Wel bourded', quod the doke, 'by myn hat!
> That men shulde loven alwey causeles,
> Who can a resoun fynde or wit in that?'   (589–91)

It is absurdity itself:

> 'Ye quek!' yit seyde the doke, ful wel and fayre,
> 'There been mo sterres, God wot, than a payre!'   (594–5)

This round contempt is, of course, a blasphemy against Love's scheme of couples predestined from eternity, and as such it is sternly rebuked by 'the gentil tercelet':

> 'Now fy, cherl!' quod the gentil tercelet,
> 'Out of the donghil cam that word ful right!
> Thow canst nat seen which thyng is wel beset!
> Thow farst by love as oules don by lyght:
> The day hem blent, ful wel they se by nyght.
> Thy kynde is of so low a wrechednesse
> That what love is, thow canst nat seen ne gesse.'   (596–602)

What the tercelet may do with proper *hauteur* Chaucer himself must attempt more diplomatically when he comes to tell his *tragedye* of Troilus and Criseyde. There, too, the potential churl in his audience must be headed off from fatal incomprehension:

> 'This was a sodeyn love; how myght it be
> That she so lightly loved Troilus,
> Right for the firste syghte, *ye, parde?*'   (II 667–9)

Chaucer in this resembles his own Dame Nature,

> that alwey hadde an ere
> To murmur of the lewednesse behynde.   (519–20)

But it is not for him to echo her authoritative command ('Hold youre

---

Wel bourded that's a laugh   *ful wel and fayre* straight out   *mo sterres . . . than a payre* more stars than a pair (more than one pebble on the beach)
wel beset properly appointed   *farst by love* behave in respect of love
oules owls   *blent* blinds   *wrechednesse* baseness   *lightly* readily   *for* because of   *lewednesse* ignorant behaviour   *behynde* (those) in the background

tonges there!'). More shrewdly, he turns the tables on any wiseacre in the audience by miming his incredulity: 'ye, parde?' is the politer echo of 'Ye quek!' From it he can go onto a rebuke which, again, it is not for him to deliver *de haut en bas*. He therefore pretends wrath; but the rebuke is perhaps not the less effective:

> Now whoso seith so, mote he nevere ythe!   (II 670)

Writing in his own person, Chaucer substitutes for the Lie Direct the Quip Modest. But owlish misunderstanding ('Thow farst by love as oules don by lyght') must be countered wherever it threatens to make darkness of clear day.

In the present work, a festive poem, all ends as it began, in celebration of a world where

> nevere wolde it nyghte,
> But ay cler day to any manes syghte.   (209–10)

Nature decrees an adjournment: the formel will have her 'choys al fre' at one year's end; and everyone else is given

> his make
> By evene acord.   (667–8)

All is harmony, and so we end with song, to celebrate the victory of light over darkness. The winter is over, the sun has

> driven away the longe nyghtes blake.   (692)

It is time for the Dreamer to awake: and, in entire keeping with the dream of perfected happiness, he wakes only to turn back to his books. *Auctoritee* has won the day; happiness is the unalterable final prospect. There is no problem of ending this poem. Life is but an interlude; how better to spend it than pondering stored wisdom? The bookish servant of love is cheerfully vindicated:

> and yit I rede alwey.
> I hope, ywis, to rede so som day

---

mote may   *ythe* prosper   *By evene accord* in true harmony

> That I shal mete som thyng for to fare
> The bet, and thus to rede I nyl nat spare.   (696–9)

Such a conclusion perfectly expresses one mood, present throughout all Chaucer's work whether as a diffused tolerance or an amused scepticism, but rarely crystallised into a single poem with beginning, middle and end, and everything handsome about it. Perhaps the Franklin's Tale comes nearest to it in finish: and there is more than one connection that might be made between the two poems—if we allow for the affection which the mature Chaucer feels towards a Franklin who plays the turtle's part. The Franklin is another admirer of an ideal courtesy, a veritable poetry of behaviour. As such he is a figure touched with gentle ridicule, but he is not therefore foolish. There are noble illusions as well as contemptible ones. To admire what does not exist, except fugitively, as an 'unbought grace of life', and to project it upon the creatures of story-telling—this, so far from being inherently ridiculous, is the outward and visible sign of that quality which Chaucer reverences before all others, the 'pitee' which is the immediate response of the 'gentil hert'. I do not see that it differs from what a later poet characterised as the holiness of the heart's affections.[10] The writer's imagination finds its own beauty (and in doing so confers a new order of existence) in the most unpromising objects, including gallant illusion.

(V)

The range of Chaucer-as-Dreamer is complete. How if a story has to be told in its own right?—not, this time, re-enacted in a dream, but a story recounted by the author as a humble follower of his great predecessors? What then of hopes for

> som thyng for to fare
> The bet?

Auctoritee and *pref*, what the 'olde bokes' tell us and what we may know from our own experience (and, if only intuitively, apply to others),

---

mete dream   *bet* better   *nyl* = *ne* + *wyl* will not

may then look forever a little different. If the turning-point in Chaucer's career was to deliver himself captive to the loquacious Eagle of *The House of Fame*, then *The Parliament of Fowls* represents a moment of entire ease and balance—the first clear fulfilment of promise, as it must have seemed to those of his contemporaries who cared at all for such things. It is a poem which looks to the achievement of happiness, heartsease in an eternal land which finally welcomes even those who offend against its laws—just as the debate itself in the end sets aside dialectical energy in favour of the process of time—the whole drawn from unimpeachable (and suitably encyclopedic) sources, and rounded with a neat bow towards fashionable French excellence in verse-making.

The Dreamer, we saw, turned back to his books, in hope to dream again. In reality, Chaucer is about to awake from a dream. On the evidence of the *Parliament*, life is but an interval in a great drama of foreordained happiness, whose appointed Regent is Nature and whose endless theme is love. When the poet comes to look more closely into the experience of love he may find that life, in some instances at least, can 'seem to teach that happiness [is] but the occasional episode in a general drama of pain'.[11] The test of his insight then will be if he can admit this as truth, whatever the ultimate consolations may be, and not be tempted to create a happy ending. The pressures on the courtly poet are considerable. Two of Chaucer's poems end in the expressed hope of doing something more pleasing to his audience—and in the second of them, *Troilus and Criseyde*, it is quite explicit that the 'better' will be 'to mak in som comedye'. The artist as entertainer is one thing: but the artist as magician—one who will change true appearances, in order to confirm the audience's ritual expectation[12]—that is quite another, even though the practitioner can be sure of heartfelt approval:

> [Thou] hast this wintres wedres overshake,
> And driven away the longe nyghtes blake.

---

mak compose   *wedres* storms   *overshake* dispelled

2

THE WRITER AS DEPENDANT

Troilus and Criseyde (I)

Troilus and Criseyde has been regarded as Chaucer's 'greatest artistic achievement'.[1] If we wish to assess this verdict we must begin by asking how far Chaucer's handling of the story compares with earlier work. We may then see how far his *tragedye* is to be regarded as characteristically medieval, requiring from us some special and perhaps limiting effort of comprehension; and how far it is other than that and compels attention in its own right. These questions are explored in this and the following chapter.

(I)

The most notable set of changes constitutes what the late C. S. Lewis called the 'medievalisation' of Boccaccio's poem *Il Filostrato*.[2] In brief, this consists in amplifying the poem by dilating upon the action or situation at significant moments, to bring out its widest implications. An outstanding example occurs in Book IV, when Troilus, lamenting his lot, launches into a long discourse on fate and free-will:

> For right thus was his argument alway:
> He seyde, he nas but lorn, so weylaway!

So far, so good: but Chaucer, unlike Boccaccio, proceeds to give us the argument in detail

> For al that comth, comth by necessitee ... (IV 956–8)

---

nas (= *ne* + *was*) *but* was simply   *lorn* lost   *so weylaway* so what's the use?

—and so on for about 125 lines. The effect of this is of course to hold up the action, the sheer onward drive of events. It is also to give the fullest and most serious context for the story and its impending development. The universal scope of the debate, its application to all men—in the present as well as in the recorded time of the story—are set before us; the more forcefully because of the bias which Troilus in his misery imparts to the argument. But Chaucer does not work only by such set-pieces as this (an addition, possibly a final addition, to his original draft).[3] Elsewhere, he quietly elaborates situation and dialogue, adding analogy, proverbial saying and *exemplum*, so that the lovers and their would-be guide, Pandarus, are firmly but unobtrusively set in a world of real experience, expressed not only in extended philosophical argument but also in homely saws, tags of learning, cautionary examples. It is this which in its cumulative effect marks the essential difference from Boccaccio's handling of the story. E. T. Donaldson sums it up exactly when he speaks of turning from the clear daylight of the Italian poem to the mistiness of the English,[4] provided always we do not assume that daylight has all the advantages and mistiness is mere confusion.

For a developed instance we may take the first dialogue between Troilus and Pandarus (I 603–1008). Here Pandarus probes and Troilus is on the defensive; until, outmatched, he at last reveals the name of his beloved. The significant changes begin with Pandarus's first rejoinder. True, he hasn't done very well in love himself: but an unsuccessful man can often help others better for that very reason (625–30). So far, all is common ground between Chaucer and Boccaccio. Then, Chaucer weighs in: and we have the analogy of the whetstone (dull itself, it sharpens other things); the doctrine of contraries (which implies that happiness is best known by those who have experienced misery); and Oenone's wisdom, learned from sad experience—here Pandarus obligingly pauses:

> Yee say the lettre that she wrot, I gesse?—

but Troilus hasn't seen it, so on we go—

> herkne, it was thus . . .

---

exemplum illustrative story   *wrot* wrote   *I gesse?* I suppose?

The lesson concludes with the doctrine of the mean; secrecy, in this light, is no virtue; Niobe's tears availed nothing; and there is, when all is said, a proverb, 'Misery is helped by company'[5] (624–735). Troilus's response, however, is not very satisfactory:

> What knowe I of the queene Nyobe?
> Lat be thyne olde ensaumples, I the preye.

So Pandarus must renew the attack. Despair is a fault; what's to come is still unsure; Troilus may be suffering the hellish torments of 'Ticius' but we can't allow his untenable opinion (that there is no remedy for this particular grief); cowardice (in not speaking out) is a fault—remember the proverb, 'Uncouth, unkissed'; and cowardly repining at the woes of unrequited love is simply absurd in a mere beginner—plenty of lovers have served for twenty years without a single kiss, and thought the service itself a reward infinitely beyond their deserving (761–819). When Troilus, impressed by this, objects that Fortune is his foe, and no man can withstand her, Pandarus is in the saddle again. Fortune is common to all men; nothing special about that. Moreover, there is consolation; Fortune's wheel turns. And, anyway, the patient who wants to be cured must show the doctor his wound (820–58). With which, Pandarus's task is done, and Criseyde's name is about to be disclosed.

The cumulative effect of such passages of 'medievalisation', as Lewis calls them, is not, paradoxically, to medievalise—to put the persons and issues of the story into a setting of beliefs and attitudes which Chaucer's own listener, like the modern reader, must accept and which at once define the moral status of the protagonists and circumscribe their acts. Certainly, Chaucer moves us decisively away from 'the clear light' of Boccaccio: but that clear light plays on a wry comedy of manners. The 'mist' that descends in Chaucer's telling makes the world of the story not less but more like the world we know. If Boccaccio presents in sharp outline a world we at once recognise, Chaucer returns us to the world we actually inhabit. In it there is learned counsel, vast stores of precedent: no man need lack a guide

---

ensaumples (edifying) instances   *uncouth* unknown (not made known, undeclared)

at every turn in life's way. But we notice that this learning is deployed
with wit and subtlety by a Pandarus who is determined to bring about
another's happiness. Something of fallibility is already present in one
who is not simply an interrogator, like Boccaccio's Pandaro, but who
unshakeably believes that love—of which he admittedly knows
nothing by experience, save the experience of failure—is the highest
earthly good. The whole tenor of his argument reinforces our sense
that he will move heaven and earth to accommodate his friend. But the
particular analogy that comes home with increasing force to the reader
is the one in which the blind man is seen as an effective guide (628–30).[6]
Chaucer shows in this (and Pandarus's bending of the proverb
'Misery loves company' is an exact instance) a nice insight into
perennial human nature; the facts of experience cannot but be twisted
when we would cite them to make an unanswerable case. Elsewhere,
and on a larger scale, the same awareness is evident in that characteristically medieval fondness for comic inversion of the truth which answers
to Dante's loss of 'the good of the intellect',[7] and which Langland,
for example, reveals in the simple mistakes of the Deadly Sins ('I wende
ryflynge were restitucioun', says a repentant Avarice, and blames his
mistake on knowing 'no Frenche'[8]). Stupidity is inseparable from
moral error. In the present passage, by small and cumulative detail,
Chaucer not only establishes the character of Pandarus. He implants in
his listeners a first seed of doubt as Pandarus's unfailing resource in
argument brings Troilus to surrender. The characterisation of Troilus
follows a complementary pattern. The 'olde ensaumples' are all very
well: but what's Hecuba to him?:

> What knowe I of the queene Nyobe?

What constitutes life and energy for Pandarus is meaningless to him,
in his wretchedness. When it comes to the doctrine of long and un-
complaining service in love, the challenge that awakens Troilus is the
imputation of cowardice, 'unmanhood'. But his response is significant,
and points forward to the Troilus who will later conduct the long self-
excusing 'argument' on Predestination. Fortune, he is sure, is his special
foe; and although Pandarus, on this occasion, is able to carry him for-

---

wende thought   *ryflynge* robbery

ward, he comes as a dependant, entirely given into Pandarus's hands.

If we take this whole dialogue as an instance (one among many) of Chaucer's 'medievalisation' of his story, we must not fail to notice that it is by means of this 'medievalising' that he sets a distance between his characters and the principles they confidently assert or ruefully accept. The distance is one that, as we shall see, the teller of the story himself comes to be aware of and in the end is unable to bridge. Chaucer's initial move was away from the polished stereotypes of a wry comedy of manners. But the moralised simplicities of an accepted *tragedye*, the 'double sorwes' which the narrator can in the beginning hardly bring himself to rehearse, offer no final refuge. As the story develops in the telling we enter upon the frightening complexities of the real: and not all the *auctoritees* in the world of discourse can modify a *pref* declared by unrelenting experience.

The differences between *Il Filostrato* and Chaucer's poem may be expressed from yet another standpoint, by considering the principal persons of the two stories. Troilus, as against Boccaccio's Troilo, is an innocent in love: where Troilo can speak of past successes, Troilus can report only hearsay about lovers (I 197–203). He himself remains unmarked—until the first sight of Criseyde. Similarly, and much more important, Criseyde, unlike Griseida, is entirely ignorant of love: she must not be so much persuaded as instructed. Griseida, at first resolute in her widowhood, is stirred by the reminder that time will bear away her beauty.[9] She ends by agreeing; a mighty sigh shows her *Trafitta già*, 'already heartstruck'. She does not, she says, lack finer feeling; but the decencies must be observed.[10] We are a world away from Criseyde whose sighs are for the 'sory chaunce' that has befallen her (II 463–4). Knowing love only from the outside, she thinks that the theory of love is the reality:

> tho fond she right nought
> Of peril, why she ought afered be.
> For man may love, of possibilite,
> A womman so, his herte may tobreste,
> And she naught love ayein, but if hire leste. (II 605–9)

---

fond found   *afered* frightened   *tobreste* break asunder   *ayein* in return
but if hire leste unless she so pleases

Simplicity could go no further; but to deepen it Chaucer transfers the forebodings of the mature Griseida, already fearing the loss of her handsome lover, to an innocent who knows love only by its visible concomitants: tempestuous and harrowing scenes, vigilant censoriousness, and male inconstancy—sheer futility from beginning to end (177–98). Her conclusion is that of the would-be sensible outsider:

> How bisy, if I love, ek most I be ... (799)

The word *bisy* carries the overtone of pointlessness as well as incessant anxiety.[11] Criseyde has no conception that lovers in reality embrace these hardships. For her, it is all a world of wagging tongues and make-believe ('hem that jangle of love and dremen').

In these two lovers, then, Chaucer has taken a blank sheet on which to trace his design. Nothing of prior knowledge, actual experience in the world's ways, is present to them as a possession of their own. Their story has therefore to be traced step by step; and in the end it will not be possible to say that love has gone awry through their failings. In the end, an ultimate question cannot be evaded: if love has made shipwreck in these circumstances, why then the passion of love? Given unspoilt nature—two who were not predisposed by experience to take and develop particular attitudes towards love—the poet can confidently appeal to 'yonge, fresshe folkes'. But that is in the end; in the meantime, these two innocents abroad must be given a guide and instructor—one who, making them aware of the *auctoritees*, will also conduct them to a *pref*.

In this, the character of Pandarus, Chaucer makes his most far-reaching change from Boccaccio. From a young man, a contemporary, and a cousin of Griseida, Chaucer creates an older man, one a generation removed from the lovers, uncle to Criseyde. He adds his own distinctive touch in making Pandarus an old and unsuccessful soldier in love's wars, one who must disclaim direct experience of the high mysteries he relates: and in this Pandarus differs sharply from Pandaro —that young Trojan of exalted lineage and high valour who has in his time known the foolishness of love.[12] To express the entire divide which Chaucer's characterisation of Pandarus makes from the Italian

---

ek too, again   *most* must   *jangle* chatter   *dremen* dream

story we could put the question: what would Troilo and Griseida have
done without Pandaro? The answer is very simple. They would have
found someone else. Pandaro is there because in every properly-
conducted *amour* there has to be a go-between, one who will create
opportunities for the lovers to move from reverie to action, from
awakened desire to fulfilled passion. But if we put the same question
concerning Chaucer's pair of lovers, the answer is that we are left with
no story whatever. Without Pandarus, what should these two *know*
of love, let alone advance to its fulfilment? Pandarus is the key-figure
in the unfolding of the story: guide, philosopher and friendly traitor,
he nourishes and sustains all up to the consummation of love. Here,
again, the quality of innocence, of inexperience ripe for instruction is
all-important—and it is to be seen not only in the lovers but in their
mentor. 'He jests at scars that never felt a wound': that is young
innocence abroad. Pandarus represents something exactly complementary to it. He longs for scars who is forever disqualified from
battle.

There is a third and final aspect in which we may see the difference
between the two tellings of one story. In the colloquy between
Chaucer's Pandarus and Troilus quoted earlier, we ended at the point
where Troilus was brought to disclose Criseyde's name (I 874). Here
the difference between English and Italian becomes final and uncrossable. Whatever minor resemblances are to come, from this point
forward there is a total divide in the conception of the heroine.
Boccaccio makes Pandaro greet Griseida's name with the reflection
that she is rather circumspect (*onesta*): but he goes on to say that the
difficulty can be managed. All women are amorous in intent; it's only
fear of shame that restrains them. 'My cousin is a widow, and she has
desires: if she denied it, I wouldn't believe her.'[13] So the stage is set.
But Chaucer's Pandarus has very different grounds for hope, and a
different understanding to exact from his pupil. That it is Criseyde, he
says, is no mischance:

> To loven wel, and in a worthy place;
> The oughte nat to clepe it hap, but grace.

---

clepe call   *hap* chance

Secondly,

> sith thy lady vertuous is al,
> So foloweth it that there is som pitee
> Amonges alle thise other in general.   (I 895-6; 898-900)

Troilus is fortunate indeed; let him go down on his knees and repent.
Chaucer's decisive shift is to make Pandarus see in Criseyde's being
virtuous the solid ground for hope: for goodness must include compassion. We are a world away from Pandaro's admission that virtue is
a drawback and his confidence that it can be overcome. Chaucer
reinforces at one and the same time the high and hopeful truth and the
relationship of teacher and pupil—Troilus kneels to ask forgiveness of
the God of Love, and to submit to Pandarus's leadership. Similarly,
Pandaro's early generalisations about all women being amorous by
nature, if only a way can be found to preserve appearances, is trans-
muted into a general statement about men and women:

> Was nevere man or womman yet bigete
> That was unapt to suffren loves hete,
> Celestial, or elles love of kynde ...   (977-9)

Pandarus puts this as solemn and authoritative truth—'this have I
herd seyd of wyse lered'—and it leads again to the hope for 'some
grace' in this particular lady. 'Celestial' love is delicately—not cynically
or contemptuously—set aside; her beauty and her youth make it
inappropriate to Criseyde, at least for the present:

> It sit hire naught to ben celestial
> As yet, though that hire liste bothe and kowthe.   (983-4)

We return to the theme of the God of Love's benevolent providence:

> Love, of his goodnesse,
> Hath the converted out of wikkednesse.   (998-9)

Now Troilus's course is charted for him: from having been the worst of

---

thise other these other virtues   *bigete* begotten   *loves hete* the fire of love
Celestial spiritual   *of kynde* natural   *lered* learned (men)   *sit* fits, is
appropriate   *though that hire liste bothe and kowthe* even supposing she both
would and could

sinners he will become the strongest pillar and most formidable champion of Love's following (1000–1). In this, the conception of Troilus as the patient, not only of Pandarus's instruction, but of the forces which that instruction expounds, is completed. Troilo, under Pandaro's leading, was emboldened: Troilus, under Pandarus's ministrations, is 'converted'. It is the width of an entire tradition.

(II)

A principal difference in the overall handling of a story that ceases to be wry comedy to become painful *tragedye* is the standpoint of the narrator. Boccaccio says he will not invoke Apollo or the Muses: his tale is of the woe of Troilo for the departure of Griseida, and it comes home to the author's own sad lot, in the absence of his lady. Chaucer, on the contrary, does invoke deities, in the successive proems at each new stage of his work; and for him there is no question of experience in love. He is only 'the sorwful instrument', one who serves the servants of the God of Love—

> Ne dar to Love, for myn unliklynesse,
> Preyen for speed ...   (I 16–17)

The proems are full of interest, for they tune the audience to the kind and degree of awareness with which the author comes to each new development of his story. In this sense, as Morton Bloomfield has acutely noted,[14] 'predestination' plays a large part in our awareness— the predestined standpoint of the author upon a story whose outcome he knows, and whose appropriate responses he rehearses at the outset of each fresh bound. Here, at the beginning of the whole undertaking, it is 'a sory tale' and so 'a sory chere', an attitude of appropriate lamentation, is called for. Troilus's is an 'unsely aventure' (where the word 'unsely' has all the grave overtones of 'ill-starred', 'unpropitious', perhaps even 'accursed', and 'aventure' relates to 'ill-fortune', 'mischance', rather than a merely neutral 'happening'). The narrator, at the outset at least, is clear about the sad necessity he is under; of his own

---

unliklynesse unsuitability   *Preyen* pray   *speed* success   *sory* woeful
chere manner, demeanour

distance from the matter of love; and of the 'compassioun' the story
calls for on his part. It is his distance from the story that should be
stressed, the standpoint of a 'servant of Love's servants' performing
his priest-like duty in rehearsing this unhappy story—

> For so I hope my sowle best avaunce,
> To prey for hem that Loves servauntz be,
> And write hire wo, and lyve in charite.   (I 47–9)

This safely insulates him from any inwardness upon the story: all is
sad, unchangeable, and piteous. But by the beginning of Book II 'of
hope the kalendes bygynne': now it is time to invoke the Muse of
History, if everything is to be truly related. At the same time we are
reminded that the writer's task is to follow his authorities

> —as myn auctour seyde, so sey I.   (II 18)

Praise and blame are appropriate only to the original 'auctour', not
to his latter-day disciple. Here is an area in which the narrator has
room to manœuvre: he can disclaim final responsibility. But Chaucer
turns this to a disclaimer of insensibility. His audience must not think
that he speaks of love 'unfelyngly'. There is nothing novel about love;
and he, inexperienced as he is, is in no position to make nice distinctions—'A blynd man kan not juggen wel in hewis' (21). The narrator
has yet a third line of defence: just as language changes (he is thinking
primarily of his role as translator 'out of Latyn') so do manners,
'usage' in love. Chaucer covers the point neatly, by comic reference
to his own audience. Some of them may react to Troilus's story with
disbelief, murmuring 'so nold *I* nat love purchace'. Well, let them:
the narrator is doubly safe—in his own remoteness from the actual
experience of love; and in the relativity of *autre temps, autres mœurs*.
His sure shield is obedience to his 'auctour'; and that is what he will
persevere in, to the best of his ability:

> Myn auctour shal I folwen, if I konne.   (II 49)

On this round note the proem of Book II ends. But the matter, as we

---

kalendes first day   *juggen wel in hewis* distinguish colours   *nold* = *ne* + *wold*
wouldn't   *purchace* (set about) obtaining

shall see, is not so simple. Obedience, like patriotism, is not enough. When, in the course of this same Book, Criseyde has acknowledged the onset of love, the narrator is careful to stress that compassion is uppermost in her thoughts:

> But moost hir favour was, for his distresse
> Was al for hire, and thoughte it was a routhe
> To sleen swich oon, if that he mente trouthe.   (II 663–5)

Yet the narrator cannot be sure that the slow and complex development which he has no time to trace will be understood without cynicism; so, as in the proem, now once again he rounds on his audience. No doubt there will be wiseacres among them:

> Now myghte som envious jangle thus:
> 'This was a sodeyn love; how myght it be
> That she so lightly loved Troilus,
> Right for the firste syghte, ye, parde?'   (II 666–9)

As in the proem, premature judgment is to be forestalled if the story is to be received at its own pace and in its own development. It is the first strong indication that the narrator must exercise vigilance in the telling of his story; and as it speaks of one kind of distance from the story—determined preconception on the part of the audience—so it also reminds us, by contrast, of another distance from the story—the narrator's own initial stance. Now we see the narrator insensibly drawn in. He cannot be the mere conduit—the 'instrument', however 'sorwful' —of what he has to tell: it has to be actively guarded from misunderstanding.

By the opening of Book III, however, all is set fair. The proem apostrophises Venus and hymns her universal power:

> In hevene and helle, in erthe and salte see
> Is felt thi myght ...   (III 8–9)

She is the source of all that is noble—'fresshe and benigne'—in human behaviour, and the cause of harmony. Under her dispensation

---

favour inclination   *for* because   *routhe* pity   *sleen* kill, blight   *swich oon* such a one   *mente trouthe* was sincere   *jangle* carp   *sodeyn* sudden   *lightly* readily   *for* because of

mysteries are hidden; and for her obedient 'clerc' they can remain hidden. As before, he takes up the familiar stance—this time as a vessel, a 'naked herte', into which the Goddess may pour some tincture of the joy that lovers feel. The task is straightforward: but the aid of Calliope, muse of epic, is needed if it is to be performed aright. The narrator remains conscious of the special quality of his third book, its moment of rest between discords, and aware, at the end, of the help he has received from Venus, her son Cupid, and the Nine. His last words to them are at their leave-taking:

> That ye thus fer han deyned me to gyde,
> I kan namore, but syn that ye wol wende,
> Ye heried ben for ay withouten ende!   (III 1811–31)

It is the end of an epoch not only in the lovers' story but in the narrator's relationship with that story, a period of what will later seem untroubled happiness—as far as that is possible to mortal man. To achieve this end, the narrator frankly admits, he has omitted some small details:

> Al be that ther was som disese among,
> As to myn auctour listeth to devise.   (III 1816–17)

His audience can believe him. We have travelled all the way from the plangent ending of Book II, with its unanswered cry—

> O myghty God, what shal he seye?—

to a quiet close:

> My thridde bok now ende ich in this wyse,
> And Troilus in lust and in quiete
> Is with Criseyde, his owen herte swete.   (II 1818–20)

The narrator's involvement, a complicity which he cannot quite leave tacit, is complete.

Book IV opens with a brief proem (the shortest so far) in which

---

I kan namore, but I can only say   *syn* since   *heried* praised, honoured
disese trouble   *among* as well   *As to myn auctour listeth* as my predecessor
chooses   *devise* relate

Fortune and her wheel are brought sharply before us. Now a narrator
who hitherto saw himself as empty of feeling is all too vividly aware
of what lies in store:

> right now myn herte gynneth blede,
> And now my penne, allas! with which I write,
> Quaketh for drede of that I moste endite.   (IV 12–15)

The sources are inescapable: but they may admit of some variation in
judgment—

> how Criseyde Troilus forsook,
> Or at the leeste, how that she was *unkynde*,
> Moot hennesforth ben matere of my book . . .   (IV 15–17)

and this thought leads to one wider in scope. If the authorities should
be mistaken, the more shame on them:

> Allas! that they sholde evere cause fynde
> To speke hire harm, and if they on hire lye,
> Iwis, hemself shold han the vilanye.   (IV 19–21)

It is a step towards engagement. The narrator does not cross that
line: his allegiance is to the authorities and theirs is the final responsibility. But in raising the possibility of misrepresentation he has made
an entry for very human feelings. Now he will truly need help—
the help of the Furies and of Mars himself, the cruel forbear of the
Trojan race—to finish this fourth book, a book which must recount
Troilus's 'losse of lyf and love yfeere'. The foreboding is sadly true:
by the end of Book IV Troilus looks on Criseyde's face, in the dawn of
their parting-day,

> As he that felte dethes cares colde;   (IV 1692)

and his final state cannot be told:

> For whan he saugh that she ne myghte dwelle,
> Which that his soule out of his herte rente,
> Withouten more, out of the chaumbre he wente.   (IV 1699–1701)

---

moste must   *moot* must   *vilanye* reproach   *yfeere* together   *rente* tore

'Withouten more'; Troilus passes out of life into a kind of living death.

The end is already in sight, and the proem to Book V is correspondingly terse. No invocation now: only a reference to the Fates, to whom the persons of the story are irrevocably committed; and, by contrast, to 'gold y-tressed Phebus heighe on-lofte' and the gentle West Wind—three years of fulfilled love elapsed, and now the parting. The proem or prologue is so brief that to some it has seemed non-existent. The fact is that the story is driving all before it: and soon the references to what the 'books' say must multiply as the story comes to its unbearable climax. No leisure now for the profession of obedience to 'myn auctour'. As the *tragedye* goes forward there is a searching for what the books can be found to say to mitigate severity. For Troilus,

> certeynly in storye it is yfounde

he was never lacking

> In durryng don that longeth to a knyght.   (V 834, 837)

The narrator can find a word of his own to characterise the successful Greek—'this *sodeyn* Diomede' (1024). It may remind us of his earlier care to shield Criseyde herself from the imputation of 'a sodeyn love' (II 667–79). Certainly, the word comes with ominous force. Criseyde had earlier been made helpless by Troilus's totally unforeseen coming to her:

> Ne though men sholde smyten of hire hed,
> She kouthe nought a word aright out-brynge
> So *sodeynly*, for his *sodeyn* comynge.   (III 957–9)

But if his character is silent the narrator must still find words for her actions; and now when the climax of seduction comes, he speaks with painful honesty:

> The morwen com, and gostly for to speke,
> This Diomede is come unto Criseyde . . .

---

durryng don that longeth to a knyght daring to do what is appropriate to a Knight   *smyten of* cut off   *morwen* morning   *gostly* devoutly, solemnly

'To tell you the gospel truth'; and this taut clarity carries all before it. The narrator must not be interrupted:

> And shortly, lest that ye my tale breke . . .
> And finaly, the sothe for to seyne . . .   (1030–2; 1035)

Once that is over, the references to the books come thick and fast: 'the storie telleth us' (1037); 'in the stories elleswhere' (1044); 'the storie telleth us' (1051): and the stories themselves are prophetically envisaged by Criseyde—'thise bokes wol me shende' (1060). There are, we hear now, things the books do not tell us—as, the length of Criseyde's endurance:

> Ther is non auctor telleth it, I wene.
> Take every man now to his bokes heede;
> He shal no terme fynden, out of drede.   (V 1088–90)

We are reminded of a distinction the narrator had made some lines before. Is it true that Criseyde's love was prompted by compassion for Diomede when he was wounded by Troilus? The narrator, leaving it to the judgment of his audience, underlines the difference between what we have on report and what we may know for ourselves—

> Men seyn—I not—that she yaf hym hire herte.
> (V 1050)

'Men say; but I don't *know*.' Now the narrator's inexperience of love justifies a reticence which warns the audience, in their turn, to be on guard against confident judgment. Paradoxically, his very obedience to what the books say is itself a ground for refusing to join in the chorus of condemnation:

> Ne me ne list this sely womman chyde
> Forther than the storye wol devyse.
> Hire name, allas! is punysshed so wide,
> That for hire gilt it oughte ynough suffise.

---

sothe truth   *seyne* tell   *shende* ruin, destroy   *I wene* I believe   *terme* period
out of drede no doubt of it   *not (= ne + wot)* don't know   *me ne list* I have
no wish   *sely* 'poor'   *devyse* require, lay down   *punysshed* exposed to
suffering

The guilt need be pursued no further than the story requires: and what others have done needs no addition. If he were a free agent, it would be another matter:

> And if I myghte excuse hire any wise,
> For she so sory was for hire untrouthe,
> Iwis, I wolde excuse hire yet for routhe.   (V 1093–9)

Just as at the end of *The Book of the Duchess*, two worlds stand revealed. Doctrine, what the authorities say, is one thing; 'routhe', the natural impulse to pity, is another. That which we cannot explain away must evoke compassion. Pandarus, at the end, can find no words to mend Troilus's sorrow:

> He nought a word ayeyn to hym answerde;
> For sory of his frendes sorwe he is.   (V 1725–6)

Pandarus would undo the past: but this neither he nor his narrator can do. There is no escape from the real world. It is another question whether we can bear it:

> Swich is this world, whoso it kan byholde:
> In ech estat is litel hertes reste.
> God leve us for to take it for the beste!   (V 1748–50)

It is the first move back, from the offering of sympathy to a merely generalised acceptance—the return to a world which *auctoritee* identifies and to which all men must submit. Now the narrator moves rapidly into disclaimers. His audience must not misunderstand his purpose; he could have written not of Troilus's unhappy love but of his redoubtable feats of arms (1765–9). Let no lady think of him as having invented Criseyde's guilt. There is a lightening of tension as he asks, with the suggestion of comic helplessness,

> every gentil womman, what she be,
> That al be that Criseyde was untrewe,
> That for that gilt she be nat wroth with *me*!   (V 1773–5)

---

any wise in any way   *untrouthe* inconstancy   *Iwis* assuredly   *routhe* pity
ayeyn in reply   *leve* grant

This leads, in turn, to the warning that men as well as women are involved in all instances of infidelity. Here again the characteristic bent of the narrator is plain: pity is called for, and it is women who most need it. The release from tension carries him over into a semi-jocular commination on 'false folk'—

> God yeve hem sorwe, amen!— (V 1781)

and then, his books laid aside, he mounts the pulpit:

> this commeveth me
> To speke, and in effect yow alle I preye,
> Beth war of men, and herkneth what I seye! (V 1783-5)

It is from this serio-comic elevation that the narrator rounds off his tale and speaks a remarkable epilogue, the biggest change of all from his original.

(III)

The habitual position of a narrator before a courtly audience, as was said in the Introduction, is one of double dependence—on his audience's patience and favour, and on the *auctoritees* from whom he derives his story and whose wisdom is greatly superior to anything he can contrive. The story, then, is familiar and the appropriate attitudes towards it are equally well established. So the standpoint of a merely bookish servant of Love is wholly suitable—

> I, that God of Loves servantz serve,
> Ne dar to Love, for myn unliklynesse,
> Preyen for speed, al sholde I therfore sterve . . .

Like the narrator in *The Book of the Duchess*, and like the hapless pupil of the Eagle in *The House of Fame*, the one who tells the story is one who can know love only from the outside. This sense of 'distance and aloofness' is, as Bloomfield observes, 'the artistic correlative to the concept of predestination . . . the reader is continually forced by

---

commeveth moves   *in effect* in truth   *Beth war* beware   *unliklynesse* unsuitability   *speed* success   *sterve* die

the commentator to look at the story from the point of view of its end and from a distance'.[15] As we have seen, there is a growing and involuntary involvement of the narrator: and this is of the highest importance for what I can only call the *fidelity* of the story, its conformity neither to preconceived notions (what the 'bokes' say) nor to what the narrator himself would wish ('And if I myghte excuse hire any wise . . .'), but its being simply what it is. Unbearable though this may be, it is unalterably true, for it has come about by no one's contriving: on the contrary, it has been borne in upon a reluctant and, in the end, unhappy narrator. Reality, it turns out, is not what either established authority or human feeling would have it to be. In Troilus's final isolation, cut off even from the ministrations of a conscience-stricken Pandarus, we see

> the very world, which is the world
> Of all of us—the place where, in the end,
> We find our happiness, or not at all.

'. . . Or not at all': the alternatives are finally clear. But who can bear to look on when all comes to shipwreck?:

> Swich is this world, whoso it kan byholde.

By the end of the story, the narrator is indeed in a 'quandary'[16]; and whatever may be true of the reader, the narrator for one cannot 'byholde' 'this world'. He turns away. Side-stepping the story for a disclaimer of responsibility and a plea for understanding, he rounds back on it, almost absent-mindedly ('But yet to purpos of my rather speche'), to despatch Troilus in one concluding stanza (1800–6); and then he sets himself energetically—with a 'pounding' which, as Elizabeth Salter says, 'is meant to still questioning'[17]—to distance himself and his audience from that far-off pagan time:

> Swich fyn hath, lo, this Troilus for love!
> Swich fyn hath al his grete worthynesse!   (V 1828–9)

This scorn, an echo of Troilus's own laughter in the moment of *his* liberation, modulates into the clanging peal of the end:

Swich such   *fyn* end

> Lo here, of payens corsed olde rites!
> Lo here, what alle hire goddes may availle! . . .   (V 1849–50)

The narrator steps back. We must make what we will of 'this world'. All that is certain is that it passes—and speedily: meanwhile, man's great end remains.

It is a development very like that of the narrator of *The Book of the Duchess*. There, too, was one who began, as the narrator of *Troilus and Criseyde* begins, as an unrequited lover. One who, as the story gets under way, knows what is what in terms of authoritative doctrine, and must therefore bring some reserve to the *pref* of others' experience. One who, as the story gains hold, moves from comfortable self-possession to absorption in what is actual, and increasingly painful. In each case, the teller of the story comes to that painful awareness by way of a revealed happiness, the portrayal of what the narrator by definition cannot aspire to, love's requital. Each narrator is one who makes a crucial transition, who begins the slide away from predisposition upon the story to growing awareness of its actual force—so that the tale becomes compelling for the audience because it is seen to be deflecting the narrator from an initial poise. The first step is admiration, unaffected liking and respect for the protagonists of the story. The words of the Dreamer, 'Loo! how goodly spak thys knyght' (*BD* 529), parallel the later narrator's growth of affection for his characters.

Criseyde is first; his feelings for her become explicit in the sturdy intervention in Book II,

> Now myghte som envious jangle thus . . .   (II 666)

What the narrator says of the slow growth of love in Criseyde's heart, its working deep down, beneath the surface of due regard—

> > she gan enclyne
> To like hym first, and I have told yow whi;
> And after that, his manhod and his pyne
> Made love withinne hire herte for to myne—   (II 674–7)

all this may be applied to his own feelings for her, now declared in

---

payens pagans'   *corsed* accursed   *jangle* carp   *whi* why   *pyne* suffering
myne penetrate, tunnel

C

action, and it is strictly comparable with the effect on the Dreamer of
the description of 'goode faire White', the mourning Knight's lost
lady. There, too, growing adoration finally broke surface—in the
simple wish that she should be alive, which in the end overbore all
other knowledge.

Troilus develops more slowly. There is about him at first, as C. S.
Lewis long ago noted, some of the shadowy and anonymous quality
of the Lover, 'the mere "I" of the allegories'.[18] Literature in this age is,
we may say, by men, for men: the interest of an extended love-story
is the interest of an essay in female psychology. How will she resist,
delay, and yet ultimately yield, without offending against the great
canon, 'vertu streccheth naught hymself to shame' (I 903)? Criseyde
must be a Lady, and love must have a slow, not 'sodeyn', growth.
But the man in such stories needs only to fulfil two essential conditions.
He must be valorous; and he must be genuinely heartstruck. Boccaccio
gives the stereotype with suitable brevity:

> Dando a' pensier d'amor la notte parte,
> E'l dì co' suoi al faticoso Marte.   (iii 20)

and Chaucer characteristically expands it:

> al the while which that I yow devyse,
> This was his lif: with all his fulle myght,
> By day, he was in Martes heigh servyse,
> This is to seyn, in armes as a knyght;
> And for the more part, the longe nyght
> He lay and thoughte how that he myghte serve
> His lady best, hire thonk for to deserve.   (III 435–41)

Only thus will the lover attract respect and, subsequently, pity; and
only thus can love be an act of compassion on the part of the lady, a

---

vertu streccheth naught hymself to shame a virtue [here, pity] is not to be taken
so far as to result in shame   *Dando* etc. Giving the night-time to thoughts
of love, and the day, with his men, to toilsome war   *devyse* relate
thonk gratitude, goodwill (The primary sense 'thought'—hence 'wish', 'purpose'—is seen in the adverbial genitive *thankes* meaning 'willingly': e.g. *love
ne lordshipe/Wol noght*, his thankes, *have no felaweshipe* (I 1625–6), 'neither
love nor [any other] sovereignty will willingly admit an equal')

grace which is wholly free from conditional gift or contractual demand
—'The noble yifte of hir mercy'. Neither Troilus nor Troilo, then,
needs any great development in terms of characterisation, once the
essential requirements are fulfilled. But in fact Troilus grows under
Chaucer's hand: and in the end there is nothing that anyone can do for
him. In the depth of his misery he cannot unmake himself:

> I ne kan nor may,
> For al this world, withinne myn herte fynde
> To unloven yow a quarter of a day!   (V 1696–7)

In *Troilus and Criseyde*, as in *The Book of the Duchess*, the only
possible response is pity. Doctrine, self-possession, authoritative
insulation from the actual, begin to crumble. As Criseyde goes down
the hill, the narrator turns back to his books, away from actuality.
It is a movement very like that in the earlier poem, when the Dreamer,
beholding plain misery, sought to find in his small store some means of
greater knowledge:

> Anoon-ryght I gan fynde a tale
> To hym, to loke wher I myght ought
> Have more knowynge of hys thought.   *(BD* 536–8)

In both poems, at the end, the truth cannot be evaded. The survivor
from love's misery, one who has lived through the heaven of requited
love to reach only the hell of isolation, stands nakedly before us.
Chaucer the young Dreamer offers outright pity. The dream dissolves
—'al was doon ... the hert-huntyng': the audience is returned to
reality. There was an ending appropriate to a story which no man
invented and for which, finally, a narrator could have no responsibility. But in the ending of his *tragedye* Chaucer feels a helplessness
before the misery of his character, whom he can in no way protect.
There can be no return, as the plight of Troilus is revealed, to the
remoteness of a 'sorwful tale' requiring the decency of 'a sory chere'.
But what can be done to help this sufferer?—one who lived far off and
under a different dispensation? The gap widens; and at the last minute
the narrator leaps back to his safe present, in which there is the

---

yifte gift   *chere* manner, demeanour

steadying perspective of eternal purpose. But the energy of protest and assertion is its own testimony to the disturbance he has undergone.

Perhaps we have in this a leading instance not only of Chaucer's integrity, of the strength of his response to the reality of human experience, but of the inadequacy of the tradition he works in. Any novelist can do better, we may think: in the silent traffic with a faceless reader the author can modulate the feelings that may have begun to grow, can intervene unobtrusively, or can, if he chooses, openly move upstage of his characters, playing puppet-master, or private secretary to the President of the Immortals. But Chaucer is never very confident about omniscience; there is a grain of absurdity in most aspects of *auctoritee*, not least when the writer would seek to join its ranks. If we are to reach truth, an unmistakable *pref* (whatever we may think of it when it is revealed), then the step forward is compassion, no matter what the consequences. The narrator and his audience may lose themselves in a dream of perfected happiness: but it is the recognition of unchanged and unchangeable suffering which must bring the narrator, at least, to his testing- place.

In a later tradition of narrative there is room for prior manœuvre, for softening the shock and for speaking a prepared elegy for transitory happiness. Of course, there are pains none the less. Dumas, Roger Sharrock reminds us, came weeping from his study because he had killed Porthos.[19] But Chaucer is not precisely in that case; having no final responsibility for the existence of his characters he can have no tears of that kind. The overriding problem is helplessness in the face of foreknowledge, the fruitless wish to cancel or mitigate that fate which the writer knows to be in fact unavoidable. An exact parallel with the novel of freely invented characters can occur only in the relatively rare case of the writer adding an earlier episode to work long since published; and then perhaps something can be done to alleviate foreshadowed suffering.[20] But it comes to much the same practical problem as the one Arnold Bennett worries out, reflecting on

what T. S. Eliot and I had said, about character in fiction. A character has to be conventionalised. It must somehow form part of the pattern, or lay the design of the book . . . You can't put the whole of a character into a book . . . You must select traits . . . If you wanted to get at a total truth you'd only get a confused picture.[21]

That, precisely, is what is happening in the end of Chaucer's *tragedye*. Criseyde is the first to go. The author allows her to see herself as she will be represented; so she takes herself out of the present story and puts herself back into the 'bokes' ('O, rolled shal I ben on many a tonge!'). But no dismissal of this kind will serve for Troilus: originally a shadowy and ineffectual figure, he in the end stands out with all the authority of the real. He cannot be, to use Bennett's word, conventionalised, fitted into pattern. The traits selected turn out to be incomplete, even misleading. A 'total truth' threatens; the picture becomes confused. So Chaucer moves in haste to end the story. Something which comes as profound shock—a recognition of the uncrossable gap between author and character, and the absence of any means of palliating it—this, for the writer, is the moment of realised inadequacy. It makes for the initial uncertainty of Chaucer's disengagement, and is discharged in the sudden energy of his final ascent—on and up, away from a world in which nothing can ever be done for the sufferer.

3

TRAGEDYE AND TRAGEDY

Troilus and Criseyde (II)

I turn now to the question proposed at the outset of the last chapter. We have placed Chaucer's *Troilus and Criseyde* in relation to pre-existent versions of the story: and in doing so we have seen the narrator's growing involvement as the simplicities of external and generalised knowledge gave way to an aroused sympathy. In what sense can we speak of the whole as a tragic achievement?

It will help to prevent some misunderstanding if in speaking of medieval 'tragedy' we use the term *tragedye*—much as the form *rethorik* might serve to distinguish preoccupation with an art of fine writing from 'rhetoric' more properly considered as the art of persuasion. Modern writers on medieval *tragedye* are quick to point out that the dominant conception is the turning of Fortune's wheel—that Fortune whom the narrator apostrophised in the proem to Book IV, least reliable when she appears most constant. As such, medieval *tragedye* is not essentially concerned with the connections (whether visible or not to the sufferers) between what man is and what may befall him. It is, on the contrary, absorbed in the paradox that disaster may come upon the good. Why, we do not know: we only know that Fortune's activities are in conformity with the Divine Will. When Dante gropes after a *rationale* of her apparently purposeless activities, he is referred to the unsearchable mystery of Divine purpose. What Fortune does is secure from mortal understanding,

oltre la difension de' senni umani[1]

—beyond the limitations our knowledge would place on her. So her palpable 'cruelty' is not to be explained: it is to be endured as best we can. Any argument that would console must go beyond human life and its self-evident 'goods', to a greater good which man may not see and must therefore take on trust. The trial of faith is the archetype of Christian *tragedye*, and its philosopher is Boethius. What *tragedye* can do for the spectator is what the sufferer in reality must strive to do for himself—to see his sufferings with the detachment proper to a spectator. This, in its fullness, is the Divine prerogative: *Manet etiam spectator desuper cunctorum*.[2] An elevation of spirit of this order is the appropriate goal of the tragedy of Fortune. To achieve it as the goal of her argument, Philosophy must take her pupil out of time into an everlasting present.

Chaucer is, of course, in a special difficulty with his Pagan sufferer. Troilus cannot call upon any reserves of faith. He does not know, what the Christian can be counselled to recall, that Fortune's delight in her operations is the illusion of those who cling to belief in retributive justice. On the contrary, Troilus would lay a contract on Omnipotence:

> 'O God,' quod he, 'that oughtest taken heede
> To fortheren trouthe, and wronges to punyce,
> Whi nyltow don a vengeaunce of this vice?' (V 1706–8)

This is all that Troilus knows or can be expected to know; merit, fair dealing is all he can appeal to, as in heaven so on earth:

> But trewely, Criseyde, swete may,
> Whom I have ay with al my myght yserved,
> That ye thus doon, I have it nat deserved. (V 1720–2)

The significance of the Predestination soliloquy is clear: omnipotence must keep its bargains, or Troilus can only conclude that it has specially marked him for destruction. This is entirely human; but, as the narrator well perceives, it is a conviction which allows no escape in this life. Insight will come only with release. When the trap is sprung,

---

Manet, etc. There remains One who beholds all things from above
punyce punish   *nyltow (= ne + wilt thow)*   *may* girl

then explanations can come thick and fast. Suddenly, it is all a long way
off, in space as in time, far removed from

> the pleyn felicite
> That is in hevene above—

and, of course, all was set in a pagan dispensation, under gods who
would neither command restraint in 'thise wrecched worldes appetites'
nor even reward duteous service, 'travaille'—rascally lot that they were.
Up, up, we go, away into an empyrean where all mortal error, pagan
and Christian alike, is of no more than momentary significance.
The region attained by Philosophy's pupil in a step by step advance
must now be taken by storm.

Pathos is, of course, the distinctive excellence of *tragedye*, and it has
a double source. That disaster comes upon those who have not
deserved it, is one thing; that the disaster is only apparent, since a
greater good lies in store, is another. But if the first encourages
empathy, attachment to the victim in his blind misery, the second, if
it is to work at all, must do so by first bringing us to a different plane—
one on which we are in the truest sense spectators. The victim does
not see, but we do. This is an entire difference from what we ordinarily
call tragic experience. There, whatever insights we are given into the
workings of any sort of cosmic system, that system remains mysterious
in its final nature and bearings. We dare not assume that it is the work
of benevolent omnipotence. We may hope, and in most tragic experience we do obscurely feel, that there is some pattern of significance in
which suffering has its place, even though we may do no more than
glimpse that pattern. Perhaps the wanting is itself enough: it is at least
an offering we make to the victim. The tragic rite is sustained and
concluded by an appropriate response from the audience to the
scapegoat. But in a 'tragedy' where ultimate purpose is confidently
asserted, any richness of attachment to the sufferer is inhibited. Our
attention is upon the system, not the sufferer. We may be inspired or
consoled; but not at the spectacle of man mysteriously ennobled in
his miseries. We come to clear understanding of a providential design,

---

pleyn full, entire

in which man, for all his follies or mistreadings, has an ultimately significant place.

This holds true whether the destiny that sustains all is benevolent or cruel. Man is no longer alone. If, in the end, destiny is asserted as benevolent, we may not lament the death that demonstrates it:

> All is best, though we oft doubt
> What th'unsearchable dispose
> Of highest wisdom brings about,
> And ever best found in the close.

We are similarly inhibited when the President of the Immortals has ended his sport with Tess. Any decisive assertion upon ultimate reality, whether it finds for omnicompetent benevolence or for the workings of 'an unimpassioned, nescient will', must leave us on the nearer side of tragic involvement; for it has in large measure inhibited the essential response we must make towards the sufferer—to wish him well on a journey that goes beyond our sight. Either to see him go down, as Tess goes down, in meaningless defeat, or to watch him enskied as Troilus is, may complete a design: but it does so by finally negating our deepest attachment.

(II)

The point could be put another way. Disclosure of final design, whether benevolent or indifferent-to-cruel, claims to return us to reality. (Whether the claim is on other grounds acceptable makes no matter.) As such, it must effect a transition from art to nature, from skilful selection and manipulation of the life we can recognise to an assertion of life as it veritably is, could we but apprehend it. C. S. Lewis once suggested that 'The end of *Troilus* is the great example in our literature of pathos pure and unrelieved'.[3] The cat was out of the bag: this is life as it is, and as we would gladly forget it, if we could. This is, I think, wholly applicable to Troilus himself. Nothing is more remarkable than his advance from a relatively indistinct figure (one, at that, touched with mild ridicule) through the hapless victim of cruel Fortune, to the strong sufferer at the end, isolated in the reality of his experience from all that either Pandarus or the narrator can do to reach

him. The narrator can only give him, literally, a fighting retreat.
Simplification sets in as the figure is withdrawn from actuality; he
merges into the stereotype of doughty warrior:

> For thousandes his hondes maden deye,
> As he that was withouten any peere,
> Save Ector, in his tyme, *as I kan heere* . . .   (V 1802–4)

Troilus has been simply passed over in his misery. The last words we
hear from him are of unalterable love for Criseyde—

> yow, that doon me al this wo endure,
> Yet love I best of any creature!—

and of unyielding conviction that what has happened is wholly un-
merited—

> That ye thus doon, I have it nat deserved.   (V 1700–1; 1721)

Here is suffering which philosophy cannot console nor art relieve.
The writer can do nothing for his character but retreat. He leaves
him to die, returning in time for a strained and awkwardly jocular
funeral rite.

With Criseyde, however, the narrator's involvement runs a very
different course. In as far as she is the Lady, she must be the patient.
Love comes to her; the news is brought from the outside world; the
uncle-intermediary is unfairly advantaged; her timorous heart can
hardly admit the possibility that she is loved. All she can see is a choice
between evils; and even so she will go no further than good manners
require:

> And here I make a protestacioun,
> That in this proces if ye depper go,
> That certeynly, for no salvacioun
> Of yow, though that ye sterven bothe two,
> Though al the world on o day be my fo,
> Ne shal I nevere of hym han other routhe.   (II 484–9)

---

deye die   *peere* equal   *protestacioun* avowal   *proces* matter, business
depper deeper   *sterven* die   *routhe* pity

All this is inherent in the characterisation Chaucer gives her, in a sustained passage (II 449–97) which has no counterpart in Boccaccio and is a leading instance of that 'medievalisation' which accords a special propriety and solemnity to the characterisation of a woman as

> the ferfulleste wight
> That myghte be.   (II 450–1)

The turmoil of such a woman's feelings—and, some may think, her incapacity for adequate response—are well set out in the soliloquy that follows her sight of Troilus from above (II 651 ff.). Her first thought is that courtesy is due to him; the more so for his being the King's son. Jump with that thought comes the realisation of the harm he could do her:

> If I wolde outreliche his sighte flee,
> Peraunter he myghte have me in dispit,
> Thorugh whicch I myghte stonde in worse plit.

Her conclusion is a pathetic attempt at wordly wisdom:

> Now were I wis, me hate to purchace,
> Withouten nede ther I may stonde in grace?   (II 710–14)

Chaucer goes on to portray the changefulness of her moods. Against the attempted defiance of

> Shal I nat love, in cas if that me leste?

comes the 'cloudy thought'

> That overspradde hire brighte thoughtes alle,
> So that for feere almost she gan to falle;

and the conclusion is in the mere alternations of hope and fear:

> Than slepeth hope, and after drede awaketh;
> Now hoot, now cold . . .   (II 758, 769–70,
>   810–11)

---

ferfulleste most timorous   *wight* creature   *outreliche* entirely   *dispit* con-tempt, disregard   *plit* plight, situation   *wis* wise   *purchace* obtain

The narrator, it seems, has underlined this passive and hesitant quality of Criseyde. From the realisation that Troilus is the King's son she, characteristically, had at once inferred his power to do harm. What does not occur to her is what in fact comes about. The narrator tells us, in due time, that

> wel she felt he was to hire a wal
> Of stiel, and sheld from every displesaunce ...

Then, he continues,

> she was namore afered—

and at once adds the saving qualification—

> I mene, as fer as oughte ben requered.   (III 479–80, 482–3)

One hurdle is crossed. But the quality of an appropriate, even a necessary, hesitancy remains—a reserve which is thought proper to womankind; and since it hovers between natural timorousness and more sophisticated reluctance, we may not have heard the last of it, once 'this tyme swete' of 'concord' and 'quiet', founded upon Troilus's 'goode governaunce', is over.

These are all the marks of Chaucer's handling. What we have in his Criseyde, unlike Boccaccio's Griseida, is a sort of negative capability, in a sense very different from that intended by Keats. It is the unvarying (and wholly unprompted) disposition to see at once the difficulties, the drawbacks, the potential dangers and even the mere inconveniences, in any new turn of events. Any advice or attempted reassurance, whether from the self or from others, makes no real impression. The reality is fear, and it is fear in its least obvious and most insidious form—the fear of dispossession or dislocation, the mere terror of change set over against the wish to be left alone. This is unpromising enough for narrative art; not much can be made of a character realised in these terms. As for tragic dimension, that least of all seems in prospect. The tragic heroine, however much the patient of forces beyond her control, must at least see that some choices are more momentous

---

wal wall   *stiel* steel   *sheld* shield   *requered* necessary, appropriate

than others and that dispossession is not the worst to be feared.
But Criseyde lacks any sure sense of actuality; and so she is peculiarly
open to authoritative guidance. The guidance she gets is towards an
unreality. Pandarus and the neophyte Troilus project upon her the
dream of perfected love, in which she is to play the Lady. By little and
little Criseyde responds to the role. It is the song sung by Antigone
that first begins to form an impression of 'love'. But this is love as art
celebrates it: and the gap begins to widen between art and actuality.
Criseyde had accurately enough described love as it must appear to
any external eye:

> the mooste stormy lyf,
> Right of hymself, that evere was bigonne. (II 778-9)

Now we hear Antigone enthusiastically commending 'The parfite
blisse of love'. It is of course to be shielded from unrefined misunderstanding; such love, it must be clearly understood, is a rare and ideal
thing—

> wene ye that every wrecche woot
> The parfite blisse of love? Why, nay, iwys! (II 890-1)

Heaven (and, conversely, hell) are the only analogues: we are not to
look for evidence in actual experience. The role of Uncle Pandarus,
counselling his reluctant niece, is complemented by the niece Antigone
confidently extolling love to her aunt. For young and old alike—
'fresshe Antigone the white' and Pandarus whose 'hewe' love makes
'a-day ful ofte greene'—the matter is beyond all question. Given this
innocent and wholehearted commendation—with the assurance that
the mundane and the superbly real are to be sharply distinguished—
then Criseyde's fears are lulled:

> And ay gan love hire lasse for t'agaste
> Than it dide erst, and synken in hire herte,
> That she wex somwhat able to converte. (II 901-3)

Criseyde's most effective mentor is neither of her counsellors. It is art,
that most powerful of all persuaders.

---

hymself itself   *wene* suppose   *nay, iwys!* goodness, no!   *agaste* frighten
erst at first, formerly   *wex* grew   *converte* change (her view)

Characteristically, once the phase of uncertainty is ended, Chaucer, as he had done before (II 666–79), when Criseyde first became aware of love, again clowns his way forward. What is life without love, tra la la? For Criseyde, in her new awareness, day and night can no longer be plainly and prosaically just that. She had disguised her feelings while Antigone's counsel was sinking in, by saying simply

> Ywys, it wol be nyght as faste.   (II 898)

But it can no longer be banal 'night' for Criseyde; and the narrator, much like his own Pandarus, carries us across this particular threshold with brisk jocularity:

> The dayes honour, and the hevenes yë,
> The nyghtes foo—al this clepe I the sonne . . . (II 904–5)

Night is now the time of the nightingale's song; a time for dreaming; and in the dream love descends as irresistible force. The narrator is happy: his story has drawn clear of setbacks and reluctances. Criseyde's heart is exchanged for Troilus's—painlessly:

> Of which she nought agroos, ne nothyng smerte—

and the story can, like the eagle in this dream, itself take effortless flight:

> forth he fleigh, with herte left for herte.   (II 929–30)

It is all a dream, in 'the dede slep'. The awakening may be another matter. For the present, the narrator is immersed in his story, drawn on by the prospect of his creatures' happiness, and ready to find for them the words they cannot utter of themselves. Book II ends with an appeal to the audience to help in this task, the all-important transition the lovers must make from passive acceptance of guidance to actively fending for themselves—never more deftly put than in the narrator's cry, on Troilus's behalf:

> O myghty God, what shal he seye?   (III 1757)

---

as faste very soon   *honour* adornments, excellence   *yë* eye   *foo* foe
clepe call   *agroos* was frightened   *smerte* suffered pain   *fleigh* flew

(III)

The contrast between the high role for which lovers are cast and what
in fact they can say and do for themselves begins to declare itself in
Book III, when Troilus, struggling for the words to tell Criseyde of
his love, is required to state 'the fyn of his entente'; because, says
Criseyde,

> Yet wist I nevere wel what that he mente.   (III 126)

There is a moment's pause. Can it be true?—

> What that I mene, O swete herte deere?—

asks Troilus, wonderingly. Then immediately we are off on the beauti-
ful formalities of the love-code (II 128–47); *this* is what he meant.
Troilus has no words of his own; and neither has Criseyde. Caught
up in a region of decorous behaviour and appropriate language,
she now

> hir eyen on hym caste
> Ful esily and ful debonairly.   (III 155–7)

There is, of course, no suggestion of insincerity or affectation. The
pupils are learning the moves in the game, the steps appropriate to
'the olde daunce'. We see Troilus growing in proficiency as a lover.
He fulfils admirably the stereotype; and Chaucer is careful to spell it
out:

> And al the while which that I yow devyse,
> This was his lif: with all his fulle myght,
> By day, he was in Martes heigh servyse,
> This is to seyn, in armes as a knyght;
> And for the more part, the longe nyght
> He lay and thoughte how that he myghte serve
> His lady best, hire thonk for to deserve.   (III 435–41)

---

wist knew, could tell   *esily* softly   *debonairly* gently, graciously
Martes Mars's   *thonk* gratitude

Similarly, Criseyde's coming to the rendezvous appointed by Pandarus is stressed as an act of obedience to her uncle's wishes:

> She graunted hym, sith he hire that bisoughte,
> And, as his nece, obeyed as hire oughte.   (III 580–1)

Again, the rare planetary conjunction brings a torrential rain, something to make any woman apprehensive—

> swych a reyn from heven gan avale,
> That every maner womman that was there
> Hadde of that smoky reyn a verray feere: (III 626–8)

and Pandarus's lying is so skilful ('so like a sooth at prime face') that Criseyde's first step in acceptance is not to be wondered at:

> Considered alle thynges as they stoode,
> No wonder is, syn she did al for goode.   (III 923–4)

The approach to consummation is itself dream-like, a dream of irresistible force:

> What myghte or may the sely lark seye
> Whan that the sperhauk hath it in his foot?;   (III 1191–2)

and in Troilus's arms Criseyde is helpless—and afraid:

> Right as an aspes leef she gan to quake.   (III 1200)

All this gives a special force and relevance to Criseyde's sense of impending disaster, once the *fiat* has gone forth. A separate existence is unthinkable:

> How sholde I lyve, if that I from him twynne? ...
>
> What is Criseyde worth, from Troilus?
> How sholde a plaunte or lyves creature
> Lyve withouten his kynde noriture?   (IV 758, 766–8)

Griseida laments, too: but the metaphor of 'kynde noriture' is all

---

avale fall   *smoky* misty   *verray feere* real alarm   *sely* poor, hapless
sperhauk sparrow-hawk   *aspes* aspen   *quake* tremble   *lyves* living
kynde natural, proper   *noriture* sustenance

Chaucer's own, and it most aptly expresses the irreversible development that has taken place. Pandarus's husbandry is at an end; now
things must take a natural course. So the narrator is sadly conscious
that any attempt to 'discryven ... hire hevynesse' would be inadequate;
real things are taking on their own distinctive shape and inevitable
movement. In the image he employs the narrator pays significant
tribute to the maturity of the actual over any representation of it. Any
attempt by the writer would

> childisshly deface
> Hire heigh compleynte ...   (IV 804–5)

The *occupatio* is, of course, appropriate; both Boccaccio and Chaucer
offer the same disclaimer at this point. But, once again, Chaucer has
taken his own distinctive path. The metaphor of childish inadequacy
goes beyond anything in his source. Humility of this order is the
sign that the story is getting out of hand—so much so that, eventually,
the narrator can be no more than a mediator, invoking a shared
sympathy for that which he is unable to describe. The lovers' utter
misery cannot be portrayed: instead, the narrator's feelings are projected, enlisting compassion on the largest scale:

> in this world ther nys so hard an herte
> That nolde han rewed on hire peynes smerte.   (IV 1140–1)

More and more, the lovers must do for each other what neither Pandarus nor the narrator can do for them.

Criseyde's attempt to hearten Troilus (IV 1254–1414) begins with
the admission that it is an improvisation, something that has come into
her head which she now speaks without further reflection:

> I am a womman, as ful wel ye woot,
> And as I am avysed sodeynly,
> So wol I telle yow, whil it is hoot ...

---

kevyness grief   deface spoil   nys (ne + ys) is not   nolde (ne + wolde) would
not   rewed had pity   smerte bitter, grievous   woot are aware   as I am
avysed sodeynly as I come to conclusions quickly

Increasingly a Chorus-figure, the narrator hastens to underline her sincerity:

> And treweliche, as writen wel I fynde,
> That al this thyng was seyd of good entente;
> And that hire herte trewe was and kynde
> Towardes hym, and spak right as she mente,
> And that she starf for wo neigh, whan she wente,
> And was in purpos evere to be trewe:
> *Thus writen they that of hire werkes knewe.*   (IV 1415-21)

There could be no stronger contrast with his earlier ebullience, when the tale lay firmly within his grasp—for example, in the cheerful assertiveness of the irruption at Book II 666 ff.[4] Now the tone is of careful pleading, and the climax is not an assertion of untroubled confidence ('He gat hire love, and in no sodeyn wise') but a careful reference to what the authorities report. But equally there is no question that the speech is the true expression of Criseyde's nature, her impulse to temporise, her conviction that somehow a way will be found. By the end of her speech, she sees herself bringing her father to heel; and she gives herself some very effective lines:

> 'Eke drede fond first goddes, I suppose'—
> Thus shal I seyn—and that his coward herte
> Made hym amys the goddes text to glose ...   (IV 1408-10)

It is, of course, wholly sincere: like Adam, in Raleigh's characterisation, she is lavishly sententious from the wealth of her inexperience.[5] This freedom of invention on her part is another 'childish defacing' of actuality. What the narrator begins to refuse, Criseyde seizes upon— the easy victories of innocence over reality.

Troilus proposes the only remedy for their situation. It is a desperate case, and the cure must be drastic: let them 'stele awey, and ben togidere so' (IV 1507). But Criseyde, true to her bent for temporising, can have none of it. Since it implies doubt of her constancy, she will swear loyalty, come what may: his plan, she claims, is founded on a misconception—'causeless ye suffren al this drede!' (1533). Life without friends is to her inconceivable: let him not think of it. Besides,

---

starf died   *neigh* nearly   *drede* fear   *fond* invented   *glose* interpret

what will people say? (1569–70). No, she will come to him on the tenth
day. Troilus is unconvinced, and Chaucer gives him lines that recall
the deep tranquillity of Book III—

> if it be may,
> So late us stelen privelich away;
> For evere in oon, as for to lyve in reste,
> Myn herte seyth that it wol be the best—   (IV 1600–3)

a stronger note than Troilo's plea, 'For God's sake find some way of
staying' (*Deh per Dio trova modo a rimanere*). In Troilus's words we
glimpse for the moment rest and heartsease, the deepest sense of
happiness fulfilled between man and woman, a pair that can miracu-
lously become one. It is immediately swept away in the renewed
energy of Criseyde's protest; and we end with an irony. Her earliest
reaction to the very idea of love ('How *bisy*, if I love, ek most I be',
II 799) is echoed in what are nearly her last words to Troilus:

> I am evere agast, for why men rede
> That love is thyng ay ful of *bisy* drede.   (IV 1644–5)

Here is 'the ferfulleste wight' once more: and it is an entire simplicity
that can at one and the same time fear inconstancy in the partner yet
confidently assert unchanging loyalty from the self:

> And this may lengthe of yeres naught fordo,
> Ne remuable Fortune deface.   (IV 1681–2)

The aureate language not only marks the nobility of the sentiment. It
seals the dreadful implications of what is less a promise than a challenge,
thrown down against the passage of time and the changefulness of
Fortune—the vistas in which the closing phase of the story is firmly
held. It is a stroke all Chaucer's own that this is a speech Boccaccio had
assigned to Troilo; and Chaucer adds his final touch in having Criseyde
modulate in a moment from the resounding 'lengthe of yeres', to the
pathetic briskness of meeting 'Or nyghtes ten'.

---

be may can be   *privelich* secretly   *evere in oon* constantly, invariably
agast frightened   *for why* because, wherefore   *rede* say, maintain
fordo destroy   *remuable* mutable   *deface* spoil   *Or* ere, before

In due time, Criseyde will lament, as Griseida does, that she did not fall in with Troilus's plan:

> Allas, I ne hadde trowed on youre loore,
> And went with yow, as ye me redde er this!   (V 736–7)

But, in a passage all his own, Chaucer reveals the extent of Criseyde's insight:

> On tyme ypassed wel remembred me,
> And present tyme ek koud ich wel ise,
> But future tyme, er I was in the snare,
> Koude I nat sen; that causeth now my care.   (V 746–9)

It is profoundly true. The past is real enough to Criseyde; and, we have seen, it acts as a constraint upon her present. As to the future, she has no power of envisaging it, except in the mere oscillation between the 'bisy drede' of daily existence and an unargued insistence that somehow a way forward will be found. It is that same insistence which, even at this last stage, comes unfailingly to the surface:

> But natheles, bityde what bityde,
> I shal to-morwe at nyght, be est or west,
> Out of this oost stele on som manere syde . . .   (V 750–3)

It is more positive in tone, with its over-confident assertion 'come what may', than Griseida's realistic appraisal: 'I'll do my utmost to escape from here' (*Ma mio poter farò quinci fuggirini*). Once again, words have to carry the assurance that the speaker in fact lacks. All the considerations that make this escape only a flight of fancy have been exactly stated by Criseyde two minutes before—again in a passage which is Chaucer's own (701–6). The character is, in a sense, getting out of hand: and there is nothing the narrator can do, as the fatal move downwards begins, except to give one final portrait of her (V 806–26), reminding his audience, as she stands on the brink, that

> There myghte ben no fairer creature . . .

---

trowed on trusted in   *loore* counsel, plan   *redde* advised   *koud, Koude* wasn't able, didn't know how   *bityde what bityde* come what may   *oost* host, army   *on som manere syde* on one side or the other   *myghte* could (possibly)

Could his present audience have seen her, they would have to agree

> That Paradis stood formed in hire yën.

And the narrator unobtrusively does what he can for her, in telling us that

> nevere mo ne lakked hire pite.

It is the amiable virtue, on which Pandarus, so long ago, had founded his first confidence in a wholly happy issue (I 899). But now we are reminded that pity has a debtor side. Criseyde is

> Tendre-herted, slydynge of corage.

No sooner has the narrator made the admission, than he covers it with a pretence of searching for the last factual detail:

> But trewely, I kan nat telle hire age.

Nothing, of course, could be less dependent upon his source than this portrayal. (Chaucer has in fact developed it from Boccaccio's describing Diomede at this point.) But the air of submission to authority, in the last and least important particular, marks the withdrawal of the narrator from responsibility for the story. It is a posture which, as we have seen in the previous chapter, becomes more and more frequent as the story comes to its unbearable climax. The 'olde bokes' will be consulted increasingly often; and what 'men seyn' will have to be distinguished from what the narrator can know for himself:

> Men seyn—I not—that she yaf hym hire herte.   (V 1050)

What we can be certain of—

> trewely, the storie telleth us—   (V 1051)

is Criseyde's own contribution to the 'bokes', her sadly prophetic awareness that throughout all future time she will be reviled:

---

yën eyes   *slydynge* pliant   *corage* heart, spirit   *I not (ne + wot)* I don't know

> Allas! of me unto the worldes ende,
> Shal neyther ben ywriten nor ysonge
> No good word, for thise bokes wol me shende.   (V 1058–60)

For once, Criseyde sees 'future tyme' accurately. Yet even now, at the moment of maximum clarity, she must project upon the middle distance a pathetic certainty:

> To Diomede algate I wol be trewe.   (V 1071)

It is the last instance of temporising. Her curtain line is of the same hopeless order, without the dignity of Stoicism or the pathos of entire resignation:

> But al shal passe; and thus take I my leve.   (V 1085)

Criseyde, then, is no character of fiction. Painfully, she lacks tragic stature. For her there are no peaks or valleys of decision: in her widowhood she would ask only to be left alone. But 'pitee renneth soone in gentil herte': and, given another innocent abroad in Troilus, with Pandarus as enthusiastic high priest and *metteur en scène*, her yielding to Troilus is made certain. In the end, as we have seen, both Troilus and Criseyde grow into final separateness from the code which Pandarus has delightedly expounded. It seems almost to be a law of nature in Chaucer's workmanship that doctrine must be made to capitulate if truth is to be nakedly revealed. Pandarus, in his final misery, must stay within the code and he can only pronounce sentence upon Criseyde for her 'tresoun':

> I hate, ywys, Criseyde;
> And, God woot, I wole hate hire evermore!   (V 1732–3)

But this 'evermore' is an empty thing beside Troilus's recognition that he cannot 'unlove' Criseyde even for 'a quarter of a day' (V 1696–8). Now we know that there has been a slow and steady growth of the real: the balance has shifted unobtrusively but firmly against inexperience fortified by doctrine. Chaucer at the end can do nothing for Troilus, in his unrelieved misery, but suddenly despatch him, delivering a *coup de grâce* that shatters the framework in which all has

---

shende destroy (my reputation)   *algate* at any rate

been set. But Criseyde, having fallen, and having foreseen what story-tellers will do to her, allows her present narrator some little scope. For once, a writer will not upbraid her: surely there is commination enough and to spare; and if it lay in his power to forgive her, he would gladly do so (V 1093–9). She is a 'sely womman', just as Troilus had meekly numbered himself among the 'sely Troians' (IV 1490): neither of them is any match for Greek subtlety. Nothing remains of the fairy-tale of the Knight and the Lady that Pandarus with childish joy and cleverness had created. Equally, nothing remains of 'Troilus unsely aventure', the over-simple, harrowing story on which the narrator had confidently embarked so long before.

(IV)

In this insistence on the real, the uncovenantable nature of actual experience, medieval *tragedye* is less the forerunner of any developed art of tragedy than the direct ancestor of nineteenth-century realism, the presentation of character immune to the stereotypes of moralised criticism. Criseyde is a woman, not a Lady in the romance-tradition. Her fears are real; love *is* exacting, its servants subject to 'bisy drede'. She makes mistakes and ruefully admits them; she believes that something will turn up; and she is truly sorry—afterwards. She can only foretell the future when she has put its verdict beyond all doubt. In a word, she is fallible human nature; and from her the fabric of story-telling inevitably falls away. There is no room for confident moralising —and for once a narrator perceives it, and, perceiving, is able to make some response. If we look for an exact parallel to Criseyde we shall look in vain: but we may find a complementary figure in Emma Bovary. There, it is true, is a woman invincibly subject to the illusions of romance, as Criseyde most certainly is not. But each is a woman who goes her own way, 'Farther than the storye wol devyse'; and in doing so each makes a highly unusual demand upon her narrator. Flaubert, we know, conceived Emma in hatred and contempt of *'la fausse idéalité'*—*'Haine au Almanzor comme au Jean Couteaudier! Fi des Auvergnats et des coiffeurs!'*[6] But precisely because Flaubert has

---

sely innocent, hapless *unsely* ill-starred *aventure* lot (things as they fell out)

done his work well, we see Emma as incapable of self-recognition; so the implied censure has no effect. For the twentieth-century reader Emma Bovary represents the essential human characteristic—in Jules de Gaultier's phrase, 'the power granted to man to conceive himself as other than he is'. Realism in this sense illuminates the human incapacity to grasp reality: and neither contempt nor aversion on the part of the story-teller will mend matters. This is the essential condition of a true narrative art, one in which the characters can have a life of their own. It is the only condition on which there can be an effective challenge to the writer himself, with his pre-ordaining plot and his tacit values, the more dangerously limiting in proportion as they remain undiscovered. There is only one working truth in this field, and it must apply to the writer before it can apply to his readers. He, before all others, must learn never to trust the artist in himself, but to trust the tale.[7] Chaucer's attitude to Criseyde has nothing in it of contempt; his response is apparent in the movement away from his first standpoint, that of 'Troilus unsely aventure', to his recognition of the 'sely womman' who needs no more censuring. It is the shift from a story which must list her capital offences—

> how that she forsook hym er she deyde—   (I 56)

to an explicit compassion, which would go beyond the story—if it could. There lies the entire difference. For modern readers of *Madame Bovary*, Flaubert's overtones of irony and contempt are no final barrier to an act of acceptance. For them, *tout comprendre, c'est tout pardonner*. That is a step Chaucer does not take. Criseyde remains 'untrewe': yet her story points not to condemnation of women, but to compassion—and compassion not only for men, but for women, who are most in need of it:

> N'y sey nat this al oonly for thise men,
> But moost for wommen that bitraised be
> Thorugh false folk . . .   (V 1779–81)

Chaucer cannot alter his story; and in this he is most medieval. But he can distinguish what the stories say from what he can *know*;

---

bitraised betrayed

and in the end this implied argument from experience is driven back
on his audience. In the total of instances of betrayal, those in which
women are the victims greatly preponderate: and in this spirit he looks
toward a more congenial task. Let there be an end of *tragedye*, and if
God sends strength he will write a *comedye*, a work in which things
will turn out more in conformity with expectation.

Chaucer's insight into the actualities of human suffering proceeds
from nothing less than courtesy—an actual deference to the reality
of others' experience and thus a natural, though gradual, laying aside
of preconceptions brought in all innocence to the task. His deepest
awareness springs from recognising unspoilt human nature when it
stands before him. This is, in his terms, *'le réel'*; and *'la fausse idéalité'*
is a world of confident assertion which, since it is amiable and disinterested, merits no contempt. Chaucer is well positioned, we may think,
to take this standpoint. It is something which the characteristic
medieval emphasis upon *auctoritee* versus *experience* readily engenders,
and which the status of the narrator, least because last in a whole
tradition, is peculiarly fitted to express. But if we do think so, we must
remember that other medieval writers do not take a similar stance upon
their stories; and when Henryson comes to re-tell this particular story
he expresses his best sense of discipleship to Chaucer by conscientiously
degrading Cressid. Chaucer's achievement remains unique: his *tragedye*
is, as Roger Sharrock observes, 'a great poem about human frailty and
exposedness, tender in its recognition of the limited goodness of
passionate love'.[8] We need only add that in order to reach that final
recognition we must start by sharing an innocent narrator's confidence
in the unbounded goodness, 'The parfite blisse', of love. The writer's
method is like that of *The Book of the Duchess*, where there was
doctrinaire consolation, and a rejection of it—but not before it had
done its work. Neither simply invalidated the other; consolation did
not cancel pity, nor pity render consolation void. In both poems, what
is real stands out unmistakably in the end. Neither the mourning Knight
nor Troilus can simply 'unlove'; and the steps by which we are brought
to reality are strikingly comparable. But all turns upon the presence and
sympathetic activity of a writer who in the person of dreamer or narrator
does not merely counsel, but is moved to enact, the pity and dawning
comprehension which the story, faithfully followed, in the end requires.

4

A RETURN TO AUTHORITY

The Legend of Good Women

Chaucer's *tragedye* concludes with the rueful understanding that once he has chosen his theme the writer cannot turn back. If he had undertaken to recount Troilus's martial prowess, all would have been plain sailing:

> Than wolde ich of his batailles endite.

Whatever the subject, once chosen it allows no deviation:

> But for that I to writen first bigan
> Of his love, I have seyd as I kan . . .

Other authors can be consulted for other aspects of the story:

> His worthi dedes, whoso list him heere,
> Rede Dares, he kan telle hem alle ifeere. (V 1767–71)

Obedience, we see, should confer immunity. The author cannot be *blamed* for this necessary adherence to the story: after all, he didn't invent it. It is an encouraging thought, and Chaucer at once lightens the tone, appealing to every lady who hears his tale:

> That al be that Criseyde was untrewe,
> That for that gilt she be nat wroth with me. (V 1774–5)

This anticipatory feeling of release from a harrowing story colours

---

endite write   *Dares* a writer on the Trojan War, here named as an authority
alle ifeere all together, the whole lot   *untrewe* unfaithful

the prospect of writing, with similar obedience, about those who were not 'untrewe':

> gladlier I wol write, yif yow leste,
> Penelopeës trouthe and good Alceste.   (V 1777-8)

Chaucer's last look at the present tragic matter already reaches forward to a theme of women betrayed by men. Characteristically, there is a rebound of humorous energy: he pronounces sentence with distinct relish:

> God yeve hem sorwe, amen!—

The hapless Troilus drops out of sight. Now we are dealing with the stark simplicity of predatory males—

> That with hir grete wit and subtilte
> Bytraise yow!

Already the orbit is one of stock characterisation, drawn from the ample fund of common story. This authorises the obedient narrator to pronounce judgment, in precisely the way he could not upon Criseyde, and to take up the standpoint of oracular sententiousness:

> And this commeveth me
> To speke, and in effect yow alle I preye,
> *Beth war of men*, and herkneth what I seye!   (V 1781-5)

Here is one man who will be exempt from the common reproach of his sex.

This is exactly the obverse of Chaucer's habitual standpoint as poet of love. Hitherto, he could only tell of love as something well beyond his own experience. It is a standpoint which has many possibilities, ranging from the comfortable self-possession of a doctrinaire Dreamer in *The Book of the Duchess*, through manifest eagerness to learn by *pref* (in *The House of Fame* and *The Parliament of Fowls*), to the painful realisation of uncrossable difference in the conclusion of *Troilus and Criseyde*. In all these instances, initial confidence in the

---

trouthe constancy   *wit* intelligence, cunning   *Bytraise* betray
commeveth moves   *Beth war* beware

weight of his *auctoritees*, his 'ensamples trewe and olde', has been quietly but decisively altered; and in the *tragedye* it has been all but undermined. The very ground, we have seen, begins to give beneath the narrator's feet. Very well, then: it is time to close the account. Already the painful story has receded from the narrator. Now the *tragedye* which records it is itself placed in a setting of 'alle poesye'; and the narrator's impulse to take refuge in the simplicities of authoritative pronouncement is completed in the ceremonious deference his book must observe towards the great masters.

As always, the release from tension is marked by outright fun. God send the author in good time the inspiration to complement his *tragedye* with a piece of comic writing!—

> Ther God thi makere yet, er that he dye,
> So sende myght to make in som comedye!   (V 1787–8)

The present sad story is to be 'matched' by 'making' (writing other verses); and if this matching should promote a twinge of envy in the 'litel bok'—well, let it ensure that envy begins and ends at home. Chaucer modulates from the energetic and hortatory tone of his condemnation of 'false folk', through the quiet solemnity of an author's prayer, to the amiable simplicity of cautionary words to an innocent traveller:

> But litel book, no makyng thow n'envie,
> But subgit be to alle poesye . . .

Yet in the moment of lightheartedness at impending release, Chaucer safeguards the status of his book. It is the last and therefore the least, but it is still within a noble tradition:

> And kis the steppes, wher as thow seest pace
> Virgile, Ovide, Omer, Lucan, and Stace.   (V 1789–92)

There is the final point of departure. The book is now out of the author's control, save for a perfunctory ending of the narrative and a last withdrawal from 'payens corsed olde rites'.

---

makyng poetry   *subgit* subject   *pace* pass   *payens* pagans'   *corsed* accursed

It looks like the end of the matter. But we may remember how, in the course of the *tragedye*, a distance had grown between what the old books told us, and what we might know for ourselves: and this, it had seemed quite early on, was a principle that ran from earth to heaven—and hell. Antigone—'fresshe Antigone the white'—had been quite clear on the point:

> wene ye that every wrecche woot
> The parfite blisse of love? Why, nay, iwys ... (II 890–1)

Happiness in love is the rarest of experiences. The rest of us must take its existence on trust. The analogy is obvious. How could certain knowledge come to us, save by directly interrogating the blessed, or the damned?:

> Men mosten axe at seyntes if it is
> Aught fair in hevene (why? for they kan telle),
> And axen fendes is it foul in helle.   (II 894–6)

The writer who expounds 'the parfite blisse of love' is therefore safe from any painful uncertainties. His theme is placed beyond question: and a majority of his audience will always find it 'an heven ... [his] vois to here' (II 826).

There is the genial starting-point for Chaucer's next work, a 'Seintes Legende of Cupide' or *Legend of Good Women*—untroubled assertion of what must command universal agreement:

> A thousand tymes have I herd men telle
> That ther ys joy in hevene and peyne in helle,
> And I acorde wel that it ys so ...   (*Prologue* F 1–3)[1]

So far, so good—

> But, natheles, yet wot I wel also
> That ther nis noon dwellyng in this contree,
> That eyther hath in hevene or helle ybe,
> Ne may of hit noon other weyes witen,
> But as he hath herd seyd, or founde it writen;
> For by assay ther may no man it preve.   (4–8)

---

wene suppose *woot* knows *nay, iwys* certainly not *axe at* enquire of
fendes devils *acorde wel* fully agree *wot* know *noon other weyes* by any
other means *witen* know *assay* direct experience *preve* prove

It is the clearest definition yet made of what we must receive upon authority, if we are to receive it at all. In the course of the *tragedye* there had been movements away from the confidence of the writer that his authorities covered all—and in particular that the actualities of suffering can be adequately represented. If the narrator were to try to 'discryven' Criseyde's grief at impending separation, the very attempt

> sholde make hire sorwe seme lesse
> Than that it was, and childisshly deface
> Hire heigh compleynte, and therfore ich it pace.   (IV 803–5)

Here the ordinary figure of speech (*occupatio*) is turned in an arresting way. Certainly, words will always fall short of the fact (and it is enough for Boccaccio's purpose to say so, laconically, at this point: *al fatto il dir vien meno*). The more common recourse of the medieval writer was to proclaim his own inadequacy by breaking off in attempted flight. An appeal to the superiority of his great predecessors over his own feeble attempts would convey all the more forcibly the high matter in hand, the passion or moment of crisis which is to be emphasised. Chaucer has some nice variations on formal *occupatio*; it is a device eminently suited to his art. Perhaps the best is his apostrophe to the wicked woman of the Man of Law's Tale:

> O Donegild, I ne have noon Englissh digne
> Unto thy malice and thy tirannye!

Such wickedness calls for the language of commination itself; so, in one neat movement, the narrator's inadequacy is turned to dramatic advantage:

> therfore to the feend I thee resigne;
> Lat hym enditen of thy traitorie!   (II 778–81)

The general principle of artistic decorum, 'The wordes moote be cosyn to the dede' (I 742), is adroitly used to overthrow restraint and reveal the suitably shocked narrator of a moralising tale. But in the instance from Chaucer's *tragedye* the primary contrast is not the

---

deface spoil   *pace* pass over   *occupatio* a refusal to describe (with the object of heightening)   *al fatto* etc. words fall short of the fact   *digne* fit, adequate   *feend* Devil   *enditen* write   *moote* must   *cosyn* akin

common opposition between reality and the adequacy of language
(least of all, the present poet's language, set in dutiful contrast with
that of his great predecessors). This 'childishness' is not simply that
of the neophyte writer, with all his skills to learn. It carries the hint of
the writer's occupation as an immature copying of what must lie
outside his range.

It is the darkest implication of what has hitherto been a source of
lighthearted evasion; and in the full course of the *tragedye*, as we have
seen, there is no happy issue for the writer. Compassion can have no
adequate reflection in the handling of the story itself. No readjustment
is possible: what 'the story wol devyse' is unrelenting. So the writer
side-steps, and in that mood mere obedience to story seems almost
infinitely desirable: 'gladlier I wol write, yif yow leste . . .'

(II)

Now, in the Prologue to *The Legend of Good Women*, the writer can
sail across the gap, and he does so with *élan*. The words already quoted

> For by assay ther may no man it preve . . .

are followed with round affirmation. (It is the same note of over-
assertion we heard as he reached the safe ground of distance from his
tragic story: 'God yeve him sorwe, amen!'; 'herkneth what I seye!').
Who is so foolish as to confine the possible within the limits of
experience?

> But God forbede but men shulde leve
> Wel more thing then men han seen with ye!
> Men shal not wenen every thing a lye
> But yf himself yt seeth, or elles dooth . . .

The tone of hearty asseveration is jocularly emphasised:

> For, God wot, thing is never the lasse sooth,
> Thogh every wight ne may it nat ysee.
> Bernard the monk ne saugh nat all, pardee!   (10–16)

---

yif yow leste if you wish   *leve* believe in   *with ye* by eye   *shal not*
wenen must not suppose   *a lye* illusory   *But yf* unless   *lasse* less
sooth (truth) true   *Bernard the monk* (proverbial for) the greatest wiseacre

We are back—could we but believe it—at the first morning of
Chaucer's setting forth as author. Humble, reverent, sententious, he
blandly assures us of unshakeable truth:

> Wel ought us thanne honouren and beleve
> These bokes, there we han noon other preve—

and this leads naturally into familiar self-portraiture. Once more there
appears the remote and ineffectual bookish little man—

> And as for me, though that I konne but lyte,
> On bokes for to rede I me delyte . . .   (27–30)

The opposition between what the books said and what the narrator
could *know* ('Men seyn—I not . . .') is softened into humorous
acceptance. Now it appears that all we know is, anyway, one sort or
another of expertise, special skill: so it's natural enough to turn to books
for more of the same thing, this 'konnyng'.[2] An air of positively
unctuous deference is conveyed in the polysyllabic repetitiveness of the
lines that follow, a cadenza on the theme of 'belief':

> And to hem yive I feyth and ful *credence,*
> And in myn herte have hem in *reverence*
> So hertely . . .   (31–3)

and the same jingle is heard when the narrator returns to his theme
after a digression:

> But wherfore that I spak, to yive credence
> To olde stories and doon hem reverence,
> And—

naïvely insistent, in case we should miss the point—

> that men mosten more thyng beleve
> Then men may seen at eye, or elles preve—

which modulates into the quick bathos of

> That shal I seyn, whanne that I see my tyme;
> *I may not al at-once speke in ryme.*

---

preve proof, means of testing   *konne* know (see n. 2)   *lyte* little   *I not*
(ne + wot) I don't know   *yive* give   *mosten* must

As always, sententious protestation is made to tumble down the stair; Chaucer enables us to see honest energy doing its humble best. The mockery is now well launched. Here is a returned prodigal who will outshine all who have stayed at home.

There is, however, a drawback to entire reliance upon books. They do not always say what it is confidently assumed they do say. Chaucer's own 'litel book', as we saw, was closed and sent on its way to join the tail-end of a distinguished assembly. But in the making of that book there came to be a strained loyalty to existing books; and, with it, a prevision that some among the author's audience would misconceive him as one who had found perverse satisfaction in Criseyde's being 'untrue'. He might even, though absurdly, be held responsible for her. Books therefore need intent scrutiny, as the narrator had more than once reminded us—'Take every man now to his bokes heede' (V 1089). But will they? The writer nimbly takes his revenge on an audience who are comfortably disposed to leave it to clerks to note these minutiae. No use, he implies, expecting the great ones to *read* the books they readily cite by their titles. How should authority stand if it were obliged to scan *auctoritees*? The situation comically reflects an actual difference between Chaucer and his courtly audience. They cannot be presumed to have read the books which are none the less the staple of confident allusion. The audience's favourite figure of fun is therefore the unworldly narrator, poring dutifully over 'These bokes, there we han noon other preve', and neatly reinforcing their own amused detachment when even he has to leave 'to clerkes . . . al disputison'. Intent readers may perplex themselves; *auctoritee* is not to be questioned, least of all by those who exercise actual authority.

In this light, the exalted figure who now confronts a sleeping poet may well epitomise the generality of Chaucer's own audience. The God of Love has fault to find. He does so *de haut en bas*, as the very embodiment of that authority which the poet has dared to impugn; but, in the end, genial condescension wins the day. It is all very familiar from earlier days in Chaucer's career; once more a magisterial inter-locutor reveals the poet's culpable deficiencies. But the God of Love is certainly the most formidable of such personages:

---

heede heed

D

> me thoghte his face shoon so bryghte
> That wel unnethes myghte I him beholde—   (232–3)

and it is peculiarly alarming that, for all his reputed blindness, he can see the Dreamer—and does not like what he sees:

> sternely on me he gan byholde,
> So that his loking dooth myn herte colde.   (239–40)

If it were not for the gracious lady who accompanied the God of Love —one whose beauty, significantly, is not to be found in mortal creatures—

> Half hire beaute shulde men nat fynde
> In creature that formed ys by kynde—   (245–6)

then the poet's plight would be desperate indeed. Ideal beauty is at hand—beauty which outshines even the fairest women celebrated in legend, who are yielded up by the poet in a graceful *balade*; and ideal beauty saves him from outright disaster:

> nadde comfort ben of hire presence,
> I hadde ben ded, withouten any defence,
> For drede of Loves wordes and his chere.   (278–80)

After this, no praise of woman will seem improbable. We have begun at the very summit, with a 'lady fre' who surpasses all others: truly, a 'lady sovereyne'. Love's ideal, celebrated by Antigone, had supplied for the innocent Criseyde an image of dangerous unreality. But here all is made manifest to a wide-eyed poet, who can only confess his prior ignorance of the marvel now revealed:

> And after hem coome of wymen swich a traas
> That, syn that God Adam hadde made of erthe,
> The thridde part of mankynde, or the ferthe,
> Ne wende I not by possibilitee
> Had ever in thise wide world ybee . . .

---

wel unnethes hardly at all   *sternely* severely   *by kynde* natural, mortal
nadde (= ne + hadde) had not   *withouten any defence* irresistibly   *fre* noble,
gracious   *traas* train   *syn that God . . . world ybee* I didn't think it conceivable
that a third or [even] a quarter as many people had existed in the whole world
since God fashioned Adam from the clay

And the uniting characteristic of this great throng?

> —trewe of love thise women were echon.   (285–90)

No room for argument about *that*!

But first, there is a matter to be cleared up. All very well for the poet to profess his devotion to the daisy:[3] whatever his present humility, he will be found out, and contemptuously rejected:

> Yt were better worthy, trewely,
> A worm to neghen ner my flour than thow . . .   (317–18)

The Dreamer is denounced as an enemy to Love and Love's following. He has translated the Romance of the Rose—'That is an heresye ayeins my lawe'[4]—

> of Creseyde thou hast seyd as the lyste,
> That maketh men to wommen lasse triste,
> That ben as trewe as ever was any steel.   (330, 332–4)

The G text makes explicit the real offence. Why couldn't he choose stories of faithful women?:

> answere me now to this,
> Why noldest thow as wel han seyd goodnesse
> Of wemen, as thow hast seyd wikednesse?   (G 267–9)

It is a matter for real indignation:

> Ne in alle thy bokes ne coudest thow nat fynde
> *Som* story of wemen that were goode and trewe?

The question is rhetorical. Of course he could!; everybody knows that:

> Yis, God wot, sixty bokes olde and newe
> Hast thow thyself, alle ful of storyes grete,
> That bothe Romayns and ek Grekes trete

---

better worthy more fitting   *neghen ner* draw near   *ayeins* against, contrary to
lasse triste trust less   *Why noldest (= ne + woldest) thow?* why didn't you
(wish) choose?   *coudest* could

Of sundry wemen, which lyf that they ladde,
And evere an hundred goode ageyn oon badde.
This knoweth God, and alle clerkes eke,
That usen swiche materes for to seke.   (G 273-9)

It is especially culpable in a 'clerke' to have made so perverse a choice;
and to reinforce the point the God of Love cites a few authorities.
They are 'Valerye' (of whom more in a moment); Livy; Claudian;
Jerome *adversus Jovinianum*; Ovid (*Heroides*); and Vincent of Beauvais'
encyclopedia, the *Speculum Historiale*.

Even at first glance, there seems something odd here. 'Jerome agayns
Jovynyan' is an attack on marriage which provides antifeminist
ammunition in the Wife of Bath's Prologue and in the Merchant's Tale.
True, it must admit, if grudgingly, the possibility that some good
women exist; and these are listed by that good, if somewhat silly,
woman Dorigen, in the Franklin's Tale (1355 ff.)[5] But Jerome is
hardly the strongest *auctoritee* the God of Love could appeal to—always
supposing, of course, he knows his books from the inside. Similarly,
Valerye, whom I take to be Walter Map, writes his *Epistola Valerii*
to counsel Rufinus *not* to take a wife.[6] Of course, as with Jerome, he is
obliged to concede that there are—or have been—*some* good women,
as Penelope, Lucretia, and the Sabine women. But there is no question
of his primary purpose. It is no wonder that Walter Map's *Epistola*
and Jerome's *adversus Jovinianum* are among the first three pieces in
the volume owned by that doughty clerk and anti-feminist, Jankyn,
the Wife of Bath's fifth husband. Whatever the God of Love may
suppose, the truth known to 'God, and alle clerkes eke' is not a simple
majority decision—'evere an hundred goode ageyn oon badde' (G 277).
The God of Love, we see, like any other defender of women's reputation, has no choice but to use weapons that are double-edged. It is
highly appropriate to Chaucer's purpose that the books cited in
defence of female virtue should all agree—Livy, Claudian, Ovid, and
Vincent, along with the avowed antifeminists—that there is, or at
least ought to be, such a thing; and that some of the authors should
look for it in vain in the women of actuality.

---

which what kind   *ladde* led   *ageyn* against, in proportion to   *eke* too
seke enquire into

Help is, of course, at hand. The Lady who herself is in no way to be matched 'In creature that formed ys by kynde' has a ready explanation. The poet has offended inadvertently; he is, after all, foolish (*nyce*); and he could very well have erred unreflectingly or at someone else's instigation. In any event, he's only an intermediary:

> He ne hath nat doon so grevously amys,
> To translaten that olde clerkes writen,
> As thogh that he of malice wolde enditen
> Despit of love, and had himself yt wroght.   (369–72)

It was the defence the narrator had offered in his own person at the end of his story of the 'untrewe' Criseyde:

> Ye may hire giltes in other bokes se.   (V 1776)

Now it comes from above: and with it, inevitably, comes condescension towards one who does his limited best—a best which is wholly dependent upon his *auctoritees*:

> The man hath served yow of his kunnynge,
> And furthred wel youre lawe in his makynge—

with the familiar reservation

> Al be hit that he kan nat wel endite ...   (412–14)

If we are reminded of the affable condescension of the Eagle in *The House of Fame*, the parallel is completed when the poet's meritorious works are listed. As before, they include not only longer works (*The House of Fame*, *The Book of the Duchess*, *The Parliament of Fowls*, and 'al the love of Palamon and Arcite') but also lighter celebrations of love's sway:

> many an ympne for your halydayes,
> That highten balades, roundels, virelayes.   (410–11)

As thogh that as if   *wolde* wanted, purposed   *enditen* to write   *Despit* contempt   *giltes* offences   *of his kunnynge* according to his ability   *makynge* poetry   *kan nat wel* hasn't much skill   *ympne* hymn   *halydayes* holidays (sacred festivals)   *highten* are called

But this time, since the list constitutes a sort of 'retraccioun', works of 'other holynesse' (the believed religion, as well as the religion of love) are added to make up Chaucer's virtuous total. On this plea, the God of Love relents and hands the Dreamer over to the Queen for suitable sentence.

There is one last touch: no room can be left for any disclaimer. Surrender must be unconditional. On his knee before the Queen, the Dreamer affirms his gratitude; but also his surprise:

> But trewly I wende, as in this cas,
> Naught have agilt, ne doon to love trespas ...

His purpose was surely beyond reproach:

> what so myn auctour mente,
> Algate, God woot, yt was myn entente
> To forthren trouthe in love and yt cheryce,
> And to ben war fro falsnesse and fro vice
> By swich ensample; this was my menynge.   (462–3, 470–4)

It is perhaps the last covert appeal to the actual audience to reconsider any hasty verdict on Chaucer's *tragedye*. But the answer, with fitting severity, sweeps all such reasoned argument aside:

> Lat be thyn arguynge,
> For Love ne wol nat countrepleted be
> In ryght ne wrong; and lerne that at me!   (475–7)

Let him be thankful, and apply himself to his penitential task:

> Thow hast thy grace, and hold the ryght therto.   (478)

He is to spend the 'moste partye' of his time

> In makyng of a glorious legende
> Of goode wymmen, maydenes and wyves,
> That weren trewe in lovyng *al hire lyves* ...

I wende I thought   *agilt* sinned   *trespas* transgression   *Algate* at any rate
forthren further   *cheryce* cherish   *to ben war* to put [others] on [their] guard
Lat be put aside   *countrepleted* argued against   *at* from   *hold the ryght*
therto keep your entitlement to it (i.e. don't spoil things by further argument)

No half-measures there: and the converse is equally true—

> And telle of false men that hem bytraien,
> That *al hir lyf* ne do nat but assayen
> How many women they may doon a shame.   (483–8)

The gap between theory and practice, *auctoritee* and *pref*, the unshakeable verities of Love's Court and the actual practices of mortals, is
marked by a final glance at the poet's world—and a final reminder of
his unfitness, in his own person, for direct knowledge of love:

> For in youre world that is now holde a game.
> And thogh the lyke nat a lovere bee,
> Speke wel of love; this penance yive I thee.   (489–91)

It is this penance which Chaucer, with all proper deference, undertakes.

The 'legends' themselves are, of course, unfinished; but they are
characterised by a somewhat unseemly briskness in despatching the
wicked villains; in claiming 'storyal soth' for what is told; in burles-
quing such wickedness as that of Jason, where a hue and cry is proclaimed;[7] and in a certain fussiness whether in tying up details or
peering with exaggerated detail into the source at a crucial moment—
as when Dido and Aeneas enter the cave where their love is to be
consummated:

> And shortly, from the tempest hire to save,
> She fledde hireself into a litel cave,
> And with hire wente this Eneas also,
> I not with hem if ther wente any mo;
> The autour maketh of it no mencioun.   (1224–8)

This mock-scrupulousness is the comic counterpart of the real concern
shown as the *tragedye* drew to its inevitable close. Then the narrator
appealed to others to search their books—'Take every man now to
his bokes heede'. Now he is the punctilious intermediary. Such exaggerated care is impossible to the devout poet of love; but it is exactly
consonant with bland deference. Love, we were told very firmly,

---

bytraien betray   *assayen* try (to discover)   *game* sport   *the lyke* it suits you
storyal soth historical truth   *fledde hireself* took refuge   *not (= ne + wot)*
don't know   *mo* more, others

will not be 'countrepleted'. Precisely the wrong view is that which
would take the 'Saints' Legend' *au grand sérieux*. The student will find
it, for example, in Robinson's edition, where it is argued that the
Legend needs no rescue from 'the charge of dullness': we are to put up
with veneration for Love's martyrs, however inexplicable the cult is
to us.[8] True; without the existence of that cult we could not have the
Dreamer's exaggerated submission. But having it, we can see what a
neat course Chaucer's prologue has run—from trust in old books
(which tell us of faithful women in the same confident spirit as they
assure us of heaven and hell); through a vision of heavenly beauty which
overshadows all reported story; to a pious obedience which must still
even the faintest of lingering protests before it can win the God of
Love's smile of approval. The first of many a 'trewe tale' is the
Dreamer's enthusiastic commendation of the Queen of Love. He is
tested by the King. Can he say what she is?—

> 'Nay, sire, so have I blys,
> No moore but that I see wel she is good'.

This loyal affirmation wins regal approval:

> 'That is a trewe tale, by myn hood!'
> Quod Love.   (505–8)

The world of authoritative doctrine has been set to rights; and in
the King's benign approval over an eager penitent we perhaps catch an
echo of that rejoicing over the lost soul which sustains another religion.
The courtly audience, at all events, can breathe again. Some have
thought that the incidents of the Prologue refer pretty closely to
Chaucer's own life, and, in particular, that the dream-Queen who by
the end of the Prologue is seen as Alcestis herself (whose flower is
the daisy, honoured by the Dreamer) should be identified with Anne of
Bohemia, whose death in 1394 led her husband to order the destruction
of the palace at Sheen, where she died. Whether that is so or not,
the overriding consideration is clear. Chaucer, servant of Love and of
Love's servants, *grant translateur* and re-teller of other men's stories,
is back in business—though perhaps not for long.

---

countrepleted argued against   *so have I blys* on my hope of eternal happiness
wel clearly, fully   *by myn hood!* my word, it is!

5

TALES AND TELLERS

The Canterbury Tales (I)

Criticism tends to turn with relief to *The Canterbury Tales*. Here, it seems, is wine which, blessedly, needs no bush. Whatever we may make of the dream poems, the *tragedye*, or the 'Legend of Cupid's Saints', surely we are at last on firm ground. Difficulties and puzzles may remain; but the bulk of the collection indisputably answers to Raleigh's description of 'the best of Boccaccio's stories' in being

so entirely like life that the strongest of the emotions awakened in the reader is not sympathy or antipathy, not moral approval or moral indignation, but a more primitive passion than these—the passion of curiosity.[1]

This is amply confirmed by their critical history. Chaucer's Tales have been read with admiration and imitated (if not always skilfully) in most periods between the sixteenth century and the present; and in our own century they have found their largest audience so far, through the skilful agency of Nevill Coghill, whose modernisations, originally drafted for radio, have in their paperback form become 'Chaucer' for a great host of readers. All this seems pleasingly suited to their being the concluding work of our earliest recognisable poet, and a striking confirmation of that range and fullness which was best expressed by Dryden:

He must have been a man of a most wonderful comprehensive nature, because, as it has been truly observed of him, he has taken into the compass of his *Canterbury Tales* the various manners and humours (as we now call them) of the whole English nation, in his age.[2]

D*

The tide of interest in characterisation has run irresistibly since Dryden's day; when we reach the later nineteenth century the novelist is enthroned as the supreme artist. But if we turn back from Dryden in the seventeenth century to Spenser in the sixteenth, we find Chaucer reverenced as a master of language, 'Dan *Chaucer*' ('Dan' is the title of his lordship), 'well of English undefyled'. Of course, there is prejudice in this—a conscious endeavour 'to bring again his own cleanness, our English tongue, and plainly to speak with our own terms, as our fathers did before us'.³ But the conception of Chaucer as a master-poet is dominant among his fifteenth-century admirers; and the important consideration is that for them he is the poet of courtly and amatory experience. Beside the mass of imitations of his allegorical and erotic work we can find only two attempts at the comic and realistic matter of *The Canterbury Tales* (one the work of the anonymous continuator who gives us the rough humour and unsteady rhythms of the Prologue to the Tale of Beryn, the other the dutiful labours, in the Prologue to the *Book of Thebes*, of that most assiduous of disciples, John Lydgate). Those admirers who are closest in time to Chaucer take him to be the 'rose of rethoris all', the superb poet of a courtly tradition who has shown the way to make English a fit vehicle for poetry. No question, for them, of a magically primitive purity: the language was, says Hoccleve firmly, 'ful fer from al perfeccioun Till that he cam'.

The first consideration from our present viewpoint is, however, not one of language but of what we think the poet is doing; and immediately there is apparent a great divide between earlier estimates and our own. C. S. Lewis puts it well: 'Where we see a great comedian and a profound student of human character, they saw a master of noble sentiment and a source of poetic diction'.⁴ That gets the priorities right as far as the past is concerned. What is overridingly important for a present estimate is willingness to examine our preconceptions—not only as to the kind of poet we are dealing with, but, much more, what constitutes poethood. If we take one more step back in time, to Chaucer's own age, there is some reason to suppose that what eventually declared itself as a comic and realistic bent came as a surprise, prompting a friend and fellow-poet to alter a commendation which was no longer appropriate. In the recension of his *Confessio Amantis*

Gower drops the flattering allusion to Chaucer as Venus's special poet
and disciple, with its clear injunction

> That he upon his latere age,
> To sette an ende of alle his werk,
> As he which is myn owne clerk,
> Do make his testament of love.   (VIII 2952*–5*)

What had seemed an assured progress, from the 'Ditees' and 'songes
glade' of youth to the crowning achievement 'upon his latere age' of a
'testament of love', was no longer so clear. We, of course, in the
twentieth century are entitled to our own views. But we must at least
start by treating it as an open question whether Chaucer's distinctive
achievement—the summit of what, as a writer, he was best fitted to
do—is represented in *The Canterbury Tales*. I stress 'an open question'.
If we can, even momentarily, take the standpoint that here is a promising poet whose career has inexplicably faltered, we may better be able
to assess the real achievement of this last phase of his writing—and
better positioned, perhaps, to evaluate what is central and continuous
in him and what marginal and even tangential. In particular, we may
be able to grasp the significance of a poet who is constitutionally
unable to finish his poems.

At all events, it should equally be an open question whether *The
Canterbury Tales* are primarily to be understood in terms of apt and
subtle characterisation. It is only a step from the words of Dryden
already quoted to the inference he goes on to draw—that dramatic
realism, a thorough-going appropriateness of tale and teller, is
Chaucer's substantial achievement:

> The matter and manner of their tales, and of their telling, are so suited to
> their different educations, humours, and callings, that each of them would
> be improper in any other mouth.

It has seemed to later critics that what Dryden could see even in terms
of 'our language, as it is now refined', and through the mist of indifferent
texts, we should be able to discern with piercing clarity: and there has
been some assiduity in relating tale (and, where appropriate, prologue

---

testament 'will', final declaration of faith

or end-link) to the teller portrayed in the General Prologue. Full-scale drama is not so much the contention as the root assumption of such a work as R. M. Lumiansky's *Of Sondry Folk*, firmly sub-titled 'The Dramatic Principle in the Canterbury Tales'.[5] Mr Lumiansky is not concerned to argue for the existence of such a principle. He assumes it, and sets himself the task of simple demonstration. But the question, it must be repeated, is open for discussion. We must approach the tales without the preconception that their *raison d'être* is the revelation of character in action.

One other assumption, in part underlying the concern with dramatic principle, should also be recognised as preconception, to be tested by examination of Chaucer's work as it in fact is. This is the conviction that underlying such a collection as *The Canterbury Tales* there must be a principle of organisation, or at least a discernible core around which the whole, if loosely, is grouped. The 'must' here is of the same order as Bertrand Bronson's 'must' when he attempts to characterise Chaucer's audience. 'Sensitive in most things, quick to catch the refinements of the subtlest humour and the finest irony, they must have been perceptive to a degree seldom attained in our own day.'[6] This is generously spoken: but is it necessarily true? Mr Bronson argues that it cannot have been otherwise—'because no poet could have gone on producing the highly socialised kind of poetry which is Chaucer's characteristic work, without the encouragement of a ready and immediate appreciation'. But is this so? Can we not conceive of a relationship between poet and audience which, putting the poet as entertainer in the circle of his social superiors, fosters in him a readiness to accept that the things which could most interest him may go substantially unregarded by his audience at large? Chaucer is always sensitive to his audience's reactions: but, on the evidence already before us in this book, it is in the largest measure a sensitivity to the possibility of *ennui*. The favourite figure is that of a bookish and ineffective Dreamer, one who stumbles upon the truth, and who must capitulate before all is made plain. His best things are for those who have ears to hear. On the surface all is plain; humour and often outright clowning are his chief resources. But within the story there are echoes for those who can catch them. It is no accident that the words 'sly', 'subtle', 'allusive' are so often pressed into service in Chaucer criticism. So

much of his work manifestly succeeds by indirection in finding
direction out. We must not, then, be in a hurry to assume that the
audience was composed of the sensitive and the discerning. On the
contrary, the God of Love in the Prologue to the 'Seintes Legende of
Cupide' would perhaps be a more appropriate representative. Certainly,
he is a caricature. But some essential characteristics of aristocratic
hauteur have gone into his making: and the fact that Chaucer's audience
can perceive the broad joke is alas! no evidence that the actual condition
is curable. However confident we wish to be about all such preconceptions there is only one 'must' to be applied. They must all be set aside
if we are fairly to confront the evidence, 'to see the object as in itself
it really is'.

(I)

Any discussion of the coherence of the Tales should properly begin,
and perhaps may end, with the plain recognition that the work is
unfinished. We must lay aside from further consideration such small
discrepancies as, for example, the Second Nun referring to herself as
'I, unworthy *sone* of Eve', or the purely literary apology offered to
'yow that reden that I write' (VIII 62, 78). With this we may compare
the 'write' of the Knight's Tale (I 1201) or the Man of Law's declaration
'I speke in prose' before launching into his verse-tale (II 961). These
are no more than signs that the process of adaptation is not complete.
Yet they point in a certain direction. The story of St Cecilia, which
bears the marks of relative immaturity, struck Chaucer as suitable for
his new project. All that is needful is a woman religious to narrate it.
Who the second Nun is, in any sense of distinct characterisation, we do
not know. Similarly, we can see that the Man of Law was originally
the assigned narrator of a prose piece; and it is a fair guess, from his
prologue lamenting the 'hateful harm, condicion of poverte', that it
was to have been the popular *de Contemptu Mundi* which we know
(from the G Prologue to the *Legend of Good Women*) was translated
by Chaucer. In the upshot, the Man of Law gets a tale which is not

---

sone son   *reden* read   *de Contemptu Mundi* referred to as 'the Wreched
Engendrynge of Mankynde' (which translates its alternative Latin title), G414

inappropriate to his calling (and critics are quick to point out the
'judicial' tone of some—not many—of its incidental observations[7]).
But we cannot say that the account of the woes of Constance is really
related to the characterisation given us in the General Prologue: and
what the Man of Law has to say by way of modest preamble before
launching into his prologue proper is a neat characterisation of
conservative reaction to Geoffrey Chaucer—a poet who, if unskilful,
does his best to stand up for female virtue, and at least doesn't go in
for stories of unnatural vice (II 45–89). True, Chaucer joins the
seams: Harry Bailly couches his invitation in jocular talk about
'juggement' and doing one's 'devoir', and the Man of Law responds in
the same terms:

> *depardieux*, ich assente;
> To breke forward is nat myn entente.
> Biheste is dette, and I wole holde fayn
> Al my biheste, I kan no bettre sayn.
> For swich lawe as a man yeveth another wight,
> He sholde hymselven usen it, by right;
> Thus wole oure text.
>
> (II 39–45)

It is entirely in character for a lawyer. But where do we go from
there? Even when we have weighed the minutiae sometimes brought
forward, the only appropriate verdict upon dramatic principle in this
instance is 'not proven'. Whatever may be the purpose or function of
the tale in its wider context, it does not notably characterise its assigned
narrator.

A further instance of imperfect adaptation points us in the same
direction. We find the Shipman referring to the 'sely housbonde' as
one who

> moot paye,
> He moot us clothe, and he moot us arraye,
> Al for his owene worshipe richely,
> In which array we daunce jolily . . .

---

depardieux by God   *forward* agreement, contract   *biheste* undertaking
wole intend, purpose   *holde* keep to, fulfil   *fayn* gladly   *by right* in equity
Thus wole oure text that's what the precept [which he has just referred to]
requires   *moot* must   *arraye* adorn, fit out

and if the husband can't or won't meet this obligation,

> Thanne moot another payen for oure cost,
> Or lene us gold, and that is perilous.   (VII 11–14, 18–19)

We later hear of the things that all women, the narrator included, 'naturelly Desiren' (VII 173–7). Clearly, a tale designed to be told, with appropriate relish, by a female narrator has been transferred to the Shipman; and in that re-casting we must lose the verve with which a female narrator can recount a wife's sly stratagems. Again, a reasonable guess can be made as to Chaucer's original intention. Presumably he first had the Wife of Bath in mind, and reasons for his later allocating her a different tale can be gone into. But what is important, as with the Man of Law's tale, is that the present tale can be regarded as suitable to the Shipman only if we do not draw our criteria of suitability to include dramatic relevance. It is suitable because it is not unsuitable: and not the most determined search has been able to uncover closer congruence.[8] Should we say that the *mise-en-scène* is France because the Shipman of the General Prologue journeys to Bordeaux and Brittany?; or that we hear of

> a jubbe of malvesye,
> And eek another, ful of fyn vernage,   (VIII 70–1)

because of the Shipman's fondness for 'Ful many a draughte of wyn' (I 396)? Everything must be scrutinised for its dramatic suitability if we are sure that tale and teller, even in this hasty marriage, must complement each other. But if the principle does not strike us as irrefragable, we had better follow the grain and joint of each story, whether hastily assigned or not, without anxious seeking after the certainty of dramatic relevance.

(II)

There are, of course, certain tales in which there is a high degree of connection between tale and teller, and their case should be instructive. For example, there would be very general agreement about Alice,

---

lene lend   *jubbe* (large) jug   *malvesye* Malmsey   *vernage* an Italian wine

Wife of Bath. We are told in the General Prologue that 'she was
somdel deef' (I 446); and when we come to her own autobiographical
prologue we learn why, in the blow given her by her fifth husband
(III 668). Congruity of characterisation and event could not be
neater. It is the same with the Pardoner—indeed, more so. A portrait
which (uniquely in the General Prologue) opens with outright irony
and continues by dilating upon his skill in wooing money from his
audiences, prepares us for his stopping to eat and drink[9] while he
meditates upon his topic—an ironic curtain-raiser in itself:

> I moot thynke
> Upon som *honest* thyng while that I drynke.   (VI 327–8)

And so we are embarked on another autobiographical prologue, one
that reveals the tricks of the trade, and serves to soften up the audience
for the grand trick that follows—and all but succeeds. The climax of
the 'tale' proper finally disarms suspicion—

> And lo, sires, thus I preche
> And Jhesu Crist, that is our soules leche,
> So graunte yow his pardoun to receyve,
> For that is best; I wol yow nat deceyve.

It is at that moment that the never-sleeping salesman strikes:

> But, sires, o word forgat I in my tale:
> I have relikes and pardoun in my male,
> As faire as any man in Engelond,
> Which were me yeven by the popes hond.   (VI 915–22)

We need not assume that a long-laid plan is coming to its climax.
Skilled opportunism will serve as well as any other explanation:
seeing the ring of serious faces around him as he reaches his disarming
conclusion, 'I wol yow nat deceyve', the Pardoner strikes home. But
whatever we make of the Pardoner's planning, Chaucer's characterisation of him is clear. General Prologue portrait harmonises with
autobiographical prologue and the tale itself sustains and in its *dénoue-
ment* returns us to the evil eunuch whom we first met. In these two

---

somdel somewhat   deef deaf   honest thyng seemly topic,   leche physician,
healer   o one   male bag   yeven given

characterisations, then, the Wife of Bath and the Pardoner, we have the highest degree of 'dramatic' relevance—a correspondence between General Prologue portrait and subsequent autobiographical admission which the tale in turn substantiates. But nowhere else in *The Canterbury Tales* do we get this: and the reason that suggests itself is that the Wife of Bath and the Pardoner are two unusually 'fixed' characters, 'fixities and definites', to use a Coleridgean term.[10] If the Pardoner is not quite as Kittredge described him, the one lost soul among the Canterbury pilgrims,[11] he is certainly drawn all one way, without redeeming feature. The crooked Pardoner, or *Quaestor* (who might be a layman authorised for this work), was, we know from many sources, the depth of contemporary evil (and is, we may think, the height of perennial impudence). Where can Liar go in *Piers Plowman*, to seek shelter from the King's officers? Only to the Pardoners who take him in and make him their man.[12] And though successive Popes had reprobated the practice, indulgences that purportedly released the purchaser *a pena et a culpa* (release from not merely the punishment but even the guilt of sin) were still in vogue—sufficiently so to stimulate the dazzling paradox that the virtuous Plowman of Langland's *Visio* should be sent one. *Piers Plowman* goes on to show that potential Christian achievement lies well beyond the scope of ordinary 'indulgences', let alone the fake wares offered by the professional *Quaestors*, those who trade 'pardoun for pens, poundmel aboute'. But there is no changing them in their brazen effrontery. Chaucer's General Prologue ends its portraiture not with any still, sad music of humanity but with the brash din of an 'offertorie' preluding the lucrative harangue:

> Therefore he song the murierly and loude.   (I 714)

The Wife of Bath is another kind of fixed characterisation, one peculiarly to medieval taste. Her role is that of unteachable human nature, the voice of unambiguous *pref* over against the many (and sometimes varying) voices of *auctoritee*. Her qualifications to be a fount of wisdom on marriage are given in the General Prologue and amplified in her own autobiographical prologue. She is herself an

---

pens pence, cash   *poundmel* pounds-worths at a time   *aboute* in exchange

auctoritee—by *pref.* Gordian knots are not meant to be untied:

> Experience, though noon auctoritee
> Were in this world, is right ynogh for me
> To speke of wo that is in mariage.   (III 1–3)

As such, she occupies a central and honoured place in a holiday poem. She is the Fool of the company, in the traditional acceptance that workaday truth is to be turned upside down. So she is kept in motion. The Clerk—the accredited representative of learned *auctoritee*—bows to her rule. Heaven forbid anyone should look for patient Griseldas nowadays! Much better to forget all 'ernestful matere' and end with a song, to acknowledge the Wife of Bath's 'heigh maistrie', her unquestioned authority in marriage and all things concerned with marriage. The Clerk's capitulation is adroitly phrased. The wife of the story had triumphantly proclaimed over her submissive knight 'Thanne have I gete of yow maistrie'. Now a clerk in his turn yields. *Auctoritee* defers to *experience*—but with the ironic reservation 'elles were it scathe', which implies 'pity it can't be like that' (IV 1170–2). In this the Clerk has improved upon the lead given by the Friar, impatient to be at the Summoner. He, too, had done mock-reverence before this redoubtable authority:

> 'Dame', quod he, 'God yeve yow right good lyf!
> Ye han heer touched, also moot I thee,
> In scole-matere greet difficultee . . .'   (III 1270–2)

The Friar has seen the drift of her arguments. But, unlike the Clerk, he is minded to keep 'game' and learned matter separate:

> lete auctoritees, on Goddes name,
> To prechyng and to scole eek of clergye.   (III 1276–7)

The Friar's 'game' is all too simple: it is to mock Summoners as, each and every one,

> a rennere up and doun
> With mandementz for fornicacioun.   (III 1283–4)

---

right ynogh quite sufficient   *also moot I thee* (as may I thrive) bless my soul!
In scole-matere greet difficultee very difficult scholastic questions
lete . . . To prechyng and to scole eek of clergye leave them to the learned, to sermonise and debate upon   *rennere* runner   *mandementz* summonses

The Friar has no time for debate. But the Clerk louts low, and handsomely gives the Wife the victory. Victorious she remains, an undisputed authority on marriage, referred to, one supposes, by Harry
Bailly when he glances at those present who could tell a tale if a
husband were indiscreet (IV 2435–8); and openly cited (in disarmingly
surrealistic fashion) by a character in the Merchant's Tale (IV 1685–7).
Hers is the rule of unreason. She is carnival Queen for a day that has
lasted six centuries.

(III)

If close congruence of teller and tale is relatively rare, we may ask
what kinds of mechanism, ways of evoking one story upon another,
are there in the Tales taken as a whole? Two can be distinguished at
once: type-casting by professional rivalry, and the engineered situation.
The first relates more to the Tales considered primarily as a sequence
of stories, without particular reference to considerations of time and
place; the second, to the enveloping narrative, movement along the
road to Canterbury and the interaction of the pilgrims. The first deals
in a common stock of agreed differences and involves no surprises; the
second is productive of unexpected reactions, situations which are not
foreseeable and which call for a degree of apparent improvisation (in
which the author, appropriately, shares, as a fellow-pilgrim). Taken
together, they make an agreeable working recipe for 'unity in diversity'.

The first group is seen in settled professional rivalries, the antagon-
isms that naturally lie between Miller and Reeve, Friar and Summoner.
No one will make a peace between these sets of traditional opponents.
Each story will have as a primary aim the scoring of a redoubtable
blow: each rejoinder will try not to mitigate, but to counter-attack.
'Thus have I quyt the Millere in my tale' is the Reeve's unsubtle
form of the Summoner's parting shot:

> The lord, the lady, and ech man, *save the frere,*
> Seyde that Jankyn spak, in this matere,
> As wel as Euclide dide or Ptholomee. (III 2287–9)

(Invincible stupidity is the real characteristic of the would-be clever

---

quyt paid back

friars. Where the Reeve is heavily explicit, the Summoner scores his point by smugly refusing to underline it.) These tales of professional rivalry naturally fall into the class of *fabliau*—they are comic and realistic, leading to climaxes which come with the impact of surprise, as mounting complication is neatly brought to its total, or swiftly side-stepped. Farce is their natural element, the springing of the trap or the sudden avalanche which finds the victim all unaware, pre-occupied as he is with what he takes to be his good. In the Miller's Tale, the common characteristic of the two dupes, layman and clerk, is credulity; but neither is altruistic. The carpenter sees himself sur-viving the second Flood to be one of the lords of the new creation (I 3581–2); and 'amorous Absolon', the parish-clerk, knowing himself 'a lord at all degrees', speaks the language of aristocratic refinement: 'Lemman, thy grace, and sweete bryd, thyn oore!' (I 3724–6). These characters derive their self-destroying energy from that older associ-ation between moral error and the 'loss of intellect' which sanctions the link between the inherently contemptible and the outrightly absurd. By the same token ('Experience, though noon auctoritee . . .'), the rough justice of this world will sometimes do all that is necessary to confound the arrogant and even things out all round:

> Thus swyved was this carpenteris wyf,
> For al his kepyng and his jalousye;
> And Absolon hath kist hir nether ye;
> And Nicholas is scalded in the towte.
> This tale is doon, and God save all the rowte!   (I 3850–4)

The Reeve's Tale is simpler in structure; a grasping Miller is out-manœuvred, but accidents in the dark, rather than cunning contrivance, bring about his physical downfall:

> by the wal a staf she foond anon,
> And saugh a litel shymeryng of a light,
> For at an hole in shoon the moone bright.   (I 4296–8)

These gropings in half-light are very different from the clear conse-

---

at all degrees in every respect   *Lemman* sweetheart, 'Lady mine'   *bryd* fair lady   *oore* mercy, yielding   *For* despite   *towte* rump   *staf* staff

quentiality of the Miller's Tale, where action and reaction are instantaneous:

> He sit hym up withouten wordes mo,
> And with his ax he smoot the corde atwo,
> And doun gooth al.   (I 3819–21)

But both the Tales in this pairing come by different means to triumphantly physical resolution: and on their way to it, Chaucer's art endows the narrators with some piquant skills. Donaldson has dealt acutely with the affected language which is used in the Miller's Tale to point up bucolic reality[13]—never more strikingly than in the contrast between high-flown locution and homely monosyllabic phrase when illusion is about to be dealt its death-blow:

> 'Lemman, thy grace, and sweete bryd, thyn oore!'
> The wyndow she undoth, and that in haste.
> 'Have do,' quod she, 'com of, and speed the faste . . .'   (A 3726–8)

The mimicry these lines alone require constitutes an oral narrator's *tour de force*. He must render a churl (the Miller) imitating a village dandy cut short by a village girl. Similarly, in the Northern speech of the two clerks of the Reeve's tale, there is an exact sense of what is necessary to establish character and mood, and at the same time the representation is uncannily accurate in philological terms. Chaucer's achievement is 'not mere popular ideas of dialect: he gives the genuine thing even if he is careful to give his audience certain obvious features that they were accustomed to regard as funny'.[14] Equally firm is his grasp upon pace and dramatic episode. When John and Aleyn are to be, manifestly, 'sely clerkes', who 'rennen up and doun' then a gabble of ineffective cries is heard:

> 'Keep! keep! stand! jossa, warderere,
> Ga whistle thou, and I shal kepe hym heere!'   (A 4101–2)

Conversely, a muddled man pulls himself together with painful simplicity:

---

com of come on   *speed the faste* get a move on   *sely clerkes* simple students
jossa, warderere down! look out behind you!   *Ga* go

> 'By God', thoughte he, 'al wrang I have mysgon.
> Myn heed is toty of my swynk to-nyght.'   (A 4252–3)

Chaucer can give these two instances of *fabliau* a full range of
realistic vocal effect, for the *fabliau* is sharply distinct from other
narrative forms in not allowing rhetorical elaboration (save, of course,
for incidental satirical purpose). In this respect, it is narrative art as
we ordinarily conceive it. The pace is rapid, the effects cumulative;
every couplet adds something to characterisation or situation. The
same is true of the other two leading instances of *fabliau*, the tales of
Friar and Summoner. As before, traditional enemies are ready to fly
at each other's throat, and snarls are exchanged at the end of the Wife
of Bath's Prologue. The delay seems to have had the effect of crystallis-
ing free-wheeling enmity into exact professional slander. When the
Friar's opportunity comes to open fire there is a deadly coolness in his
handling of the tale. The vileness of all summoners is entirely taken
as read, and spluttering interruption by the Summoner actually present
is calmly ignored:

> 'This false theef, this somonour', quod the Frere,
> 'Hadd alwey bawdes redy to his hond,
> As any hauk to lure in Engelond . . .'   (III 1338–40)

This, the actual situation of the two rival Pilgrims, is neatly transposed
into the Friar's tale, where a summoner has to discover the truth from
an interlocutor who is in unhurried possession of it. The victim
eagerly seeks closer acquaintance:

> 'Wel be we met, by God and by Seint Jame!
> But, leeve brother, tel me thanne thy name',
> Quod this sumonour. In this meene while
> This yeman gan a litel for to smyle . . .   (III 1443–6)

The Friar-narrator, like the 'yeman' of his story, has the real Summoner
at his mercy; so the summoner of the story is not spared the role of
stupid questioner, unable to profit by the polished little lecture he is

---

mysgon gone awry *heed* head *toty* dizzy *of* from *swynk* hard work
bawdes go-betweens *As any hauk* just like the devices used to lure any hawk
Jame James *leeve* dear *yeman* yeoman

given because too dull to see the all-important distinction between word and intent—a thrust at those whose trade is in misrepresentation. To complete the rout of his opponent, the Friar addresses himself, more in sorrow than in anger, to his distinguished congregation, explaining that, but for 'this Somnour heere', he could dilate upon hell's pains; and he concludes magnanimously with a prayer for the misguided:

> that thise somonours hem repente
> Of hir mysdedes, er that the feend hem hente!

It is a devastating performance, delivered very much *de haut en bas*, from one who claims to be a real theologian and churchman—had he but other world enough and time—to the noble company of his intellectual peers. Nothing could be better calculated to enrage the class of stupid mere officials. The Friar succeeds:

> This Somonour in his styropes hye stood;
> Upon this Frere his herte was so wood
> That lyk an aspen leef he quook for ire.   (III 1665–7)

The Summoner's tale consequently threatens to be the very opposite of the Friar's urbane performance: and this is still in prospect at the end of his prologue—an ending strikingly different from the Friar's urbane conclusion. Where the Friar had piously wished (if it were possible) for the amendment of all summoners, the Summoner's prayer savagely excludes this particular Friar from general benediction:

> God save yow alle, save this cursed Frere!   (III 1707)

But even in his overbearing rage, the Summoner is shrewd enough to pick up the point the Friar had last made, and hurl it back. Certainly the Friar could discourse at large on hell: for who should know hell better than the friars? It's common knowledge (a trick taken from the Friar's repertoire) that

> Freres and feendes been but lyte asonder.   (III 1674)

---

feend Devil   *hente* carry them off   *upon* towards   *wood* enraged
quook quivered   *lyte* little

At once, we sense a weakness in the Friar's apparently impregnable position. If the summoner of his story was a surrogate-figure for the real Summoner, his fellow-pilgrim, can we resist asking how the other person of the story, the devil, is related to the Friar himself? No wonder the Friar is an expert on hell! Now the Reeve goes a stage farther, and it is a step which gives him the central notion of his story. The place assigned to friars is under Satan's capacious tail. Given the idea, the Summoner steadies his course: and the story that follows is, surprisingly, delivered with no less self-possession than the Friar's. Indeed, the Friar has nothing better than the sustained irony of the speeches dramatised by the Summoner. For example, the mock-hesitations of delicate greed:

> 'Now, dame,' quod he, 'now *je vous dy sanȝ doute,*
> Have I nat of a capon but the lyvere,
> And of youre softe breed nat but a shyvere,
> And after that a rosted pigges heed—
> But that I nolde no beest for me were deed—
> Than hadde I with yow hoomly suffisaunce ...   (III 1838–43)

It is all there, down to the parenthetic disclaimer—'I'd be the last to cause any trouble'—and the unctuous *bonhomie* of the concluding phrase ('enough is as good as a feast, I always say'). Or there is the searing irony of hypocrisy given its smoothly practised run:

> For, sire and dame, trusteth me right weel,
> Oure orisons been moore effectueel,
> And moore we seen of Cristes secree thynges,
> Than burel folk, although they weren kynges.
> We lyve in poverte and in abstinence,
> And burell folk in richesse and despence
> Of mete and drynke, and in hir foul delit.
> We han this worldes lust al in despit.   (III 1869–76)

This wickedly exact ear for speech is paralleled by precise observation—

---

je vous dy sanȝ doute I won't lie   *capon* fowl   *shyvere* shaving, thin slice
nolde (= ne + wolde) wouldn't wish   *deed* dead   *secree thynges* mysteries
burel lay, secular   *despence* expenditure   *foul delit* sensual gratification
han have (i.e. hold)   *lust* pleasure   *despit* contempt

> fro the bench he droof awey the cat,
> And leyde adoun his potente and his hat— (III 1775–6)

and the practised greeting for the lady of the house:

> kiste hire sweete, and chirketh as a sparwe
> With his lyppes— (III 1804–5)

There is no loophole now: it all unfolds as irresistibly as life itself. Anger has stimulated in the Summoner a wonderfully heightened awareness. Above all, he can bide his time. There is an absolute poise in the initial contrast between the practised loquacity of the friar and the laconic replies of the old man, Thomas—the perfect build-up for a swift reversal. When the friar of the story is discomfited, anger is adroitly transferred to him; and for once this smooth talker can find no words:

> He looked as it were a wilde boor;
> He grynte with his teeth, so was he wrooth.
> A sturdy paas doun to the court he gooth ... (III 2160–2)

There is a nice revenge for the actual narrator in the speechless rage of his friar; and from it he builds a beautifully comic scene—the lord of the manor peacefully at dinner confronted with a dumbfounded friar:

> Unnethes myghte the frere speke a word,
> Til atte last he seyde, 'God yow see!' (III 2168–9)

With an exact timing, the narrator pauses. Can this be our eloquent friend? The point must be taken by the audience just one moment before the lord of the manor raises his head in astonishment:

> This lord gan looke, and seide, '*Benedicitee!*
> What, frere John, what maner world is this?' (III 2170–1)

Friars, however, are not silenced for long. The Summoner re-animates

---

droof drove   *potente* staff   *sweete* sweetly   *chirketh* chirps   *sparwe* sparrow
grynte gnashed   *wrooth* enraged   *sturdy* furious   *court* manor-house
Unnethes scarcely   *see* watch over, preserve   *Benedicitee!* God bless us!
what maner world? what kind of business?

his friar with the same exactness of ear he had shown before. A first outburst draws an opening reply from the lord of the manor; but he is smoothly overriden as automatic eloquence once again settles into its habitual track:

> 'Now, maister,' quod this lord, 'I yow biseke—'
> 'No maister, sire,' quod he, 'but servitour,
> Thogh I have had in scole that honour.
> God liketh nat that "Raby" men us calle,
> Neither in market ne in youre large halle.'

It passes belief; but it is precisely true. The automatic response, the practised assertion of humility, the mechanical allusion to the Master which blandly links scriptural market-place with actual manor-house —all take the breath away. The lord of the manor has to move on— hastily it seems:

> 'No fors,' quod he, 'but tel me al youre grief.'

The narrator neatly concludes the scene by shifting the focus: now a lord concentrates with comic profundity on a churl's resourcefulness. It is a preparation for the final demonstration that all the boasted learning of friars comes to nothing in the real world.

> The lord sat stille as he were in a traunce,
> And in his hert he rolled up and doun,
> 'How hadde this cherl ymaginacioun
> To shewe swich a probleme to the frere?'   (III 2216–19)

There is apparently no ordinary solution. He must be 'demonyak': so 'Lat hym go honge hymself a devel weye!' But the Summoner has still a trick up *his* sleeve. The final rout of the pilgrim-Friar turns on proving that the churl is in fact 'no fool, ne no demonyak'. In the squire's solution we have not only an answer to the practical problem, but a solution which, exactly adapted to the nature of friars and their hierarchical niceties, proves to all that the boasted learning of a

---

in scole at the university   *Raby* Rabbi (Matt. xxiii, 7)   *No fors* never mind
ymaginacioun ingenuity   *shewe* present   *demonyak* possessed by an evil spirit
a devel weye and go to the Devil

'Euclide' or 'Ptholomee' is readily matched in the practical resource-fulness of a squire—and, of course, in the 'subtiltee And heigh wit' of a churl. Proved to all, that is 'save the frere'. No need for the Summoner to point his moral in the concluding lines. Never in the upper reaches of 'flyting' have game, set and match been so comfortably won, after so unpromising a start.

In this quartet of tales we have the *fabliau* raised to its highest pitch of possibility. Criticism is sometimes in danger of neglecting these stories, in its haste to do justice to the more intricate qualities of romance or mock-heroic, saint's legend or *exemplum*, and so on—those tales, in a word, where rhetorical elaboration is appropriate and there-fore some distance set between the modern reader's expectancy and characteristically medieval execution. Perhaps we need to remind ourselves that what can be simply formulated—in this instance, 'straight narration, designed to score off the opponent'—is not there-fore simple (much less inferior, inexact, or undemanding) in its execution. Chaucer has taken the *fabliau* and made it the perfect basis for oral narration—by a preponderance of direct speech; by accurately vocalising affectation, mechanical fluency, and regional origins; and by skill in timing, including the well-placed pause. The *fabliau* in his hands is not a poor relation among the more elaborate forms of story-telling. Had he written nothing else he would stand as an undisputed master of narrative art. These stories, in particular the Miller's and the Summoner's, have never, in their own kind, been equalled. Realism can never be the same again.

(IV)

I turn now to those tales which arise not from settled and predictable antagonism but in circumstances that could not be foreseen; and here two Pilgrims are notably manœuvred into action, the Monk and Geoffrey Chaucer, in obedience to the original 'foreward'. The Monk comes first, called upon by Harry Bailly to tell

Somewhat to quite with the Knyghtes tale   (I 3119)

---

wit intelligence   *foreward* agreement   *quite with* repay, match

But the plan miscarries in the first outburst of dissent. The Miller

> that for dronken was al pale,
> So that unnethe upon his hors he sat   (I 3120-1)

is in no mood for any civilities; and, given his head, he reveals his purpose, to chalk up a score against carpenters. The game is afoot, and the Host's choice has to go by the board until the churls are done. At what precise point in the sequence the Monk is called upon again will depend on our choice of overall order.[15] But it is clear that, after however long or short a time from his first being called upon, the Monk is summoned into action once more with the ending of Chaucer's own 'tale of Melibee'. The Host has expatiated on the actualities of marriage: his own wife doesn't at all resemble the patient Prudence of Chaucer's tale, any more than a real woman could be found to match the Clerk's Griselda. Once again, it is time to turn from edifying *auctoritee* to uncompromising actuality: and in this spirit the Host calls upon the Monk. Heavily jocular searching for a suitably dignified mode of address leads to knowing glances at the Monk's bulk—and, by an easy transition, to what may be surmised of his fleshly exploits. But the Monk is not to be drawn. It is an open question whether we are dealing with the Monk of the General Prologue or with a more genuinely dignified figure when we hear the narrator say

> This worthy Monk took al in pacience ...   (VII 1965)

and we are off on the prologue to what threatens to be an endless recital of *tragedies,*

> Of whiche I have an hundred in my celle.   (VII 1972)

Is this an instance where we are to suppose Chaucer would have drawn the threads tighter on revision? Certainly the connection with the General Prologue portrait is not obvious: and attempts to explain matters by calling in Chaucer the Pilgrim—whether we assume an offended 'sense of decorum' (so that his present comment is one of 'deferential commiseration'[16]), or go farther back and see him as having formed a mistaken first impression[17]—do not materially help.

---

for dronken because of being drunk   *unnethe* scarcely, with difficulty

On the facts as we have them, here is a juncture in the overall narrative at which the competing claims of the Host's authority and the disposition of individuals to go their own way—another sort of conflict between *auctoritee* and *pref*—confront us squarely. The Monk who suffers 'al in pacience' has taken the point of the tale about Dame Pacience: he now proceeds to test the patience of his audience. Real authority is needed to stop him—not any interruption by the Host, armed with his holiday-rule, but the displeasure of the Knight, that established keeper of the peace. Harry Bailly is quick to echo the plain man's criticism which the Knight voices. He follows the Knight's lead in asking for stories of 'joye and greet solas', but returns neatly to his first appeal in asking, this time with the right touch of deference,

> Sir, sey somwhat of huntyng, I yow preye.   (VII 2805)

Hunting or another kind of venery—it is all one, so long as it holds the promise of 'desport' or 'game'. But the Monk is not to be drawn:

> 'Nay,' quod this Monk, 'I have no lust to pleye
> Now lat another telle, as I have toold.'   (VII 2806–7)

It is time for Harry Bailly to round upon some less formidable ecclesiastic; and out of obscurity there rides the Nun's Priest, with his holiday deference to the Host and his curate-like willingness to oblige:

> 'Yis, sir,' quod he, 'yis, Hoost, so moot I go,
> But I be myrie, ywis I wol be blamed'—   (VII 2816–17)

and we are off on a tale which blends the apparent simplicities of fable with the subtleties of clerkly debate.

Harry Bailly's lack of success with the Monk follows and up to a point parallels his earlier failure with another Pilgrim, Chaucer himself. Here again, the situation is one that relates to the overall setting, and to a principle of change of mood. After the sweet solemnity of the Prioress's Tale, there is thoughtful silence:

---

solas entertainment   *no lust* no wish, inclination   *so moot I go* (lit.) as I hope to have the use of my legs   *But* unless

> every man
>
> As sobre was that wonder was to se.   (VII 691–2)

It falls to the Host to break this up: and, as he had successfully wooed the Prioress, with all decorum—

> As curteisly as it had been a mayde—   (VII 445)

now he begins to play the fool ('japen'), and picks on Chaucer as a promising target, pushing him into prominence with mock-concern for both his abstraction and his girth:

> Now war yow, sires, and lat this man have place!   (VII 699)

After the pathos of the tale of the boy-martyr, there can be no question of what the next speaker must attempt:

> Telle us a tale of myrthe, and that anoon.   (VII 706)

Harry Bailly has, unwittingly, met his match. From the two leads in his boisterous introduction, Chaucer the Pilgrim constructs all he needs for his first story. The Host's heavily jocular, mock-dignified address to the Pilgrims ('Now war yow, sires!') and the characterisation of the intended victim as someone from another world ('He semeth *elvyssh* by his contenaunce') suggest in one swift turn the stock manner and matter of the *joculator*, the market-place entertainer. Harry Bailly's 'Now war yow, sires!' is echoed by the honorific opening appeal

> Listeth, lordes, in good entent . . .

and this launches us upon the appropriate fiction of 'An elf-queene' and her notable suitor. It is all very suitable to the character of remote and ineffectual don which Harry Bailly has thrust upon Chaucer. What stories should *he* produce, in dutiful compliance with the point-blank demand—'Telle us a tale of myrthe, and that anoon'—save something he 'lerned longe agoon'?

Readers who are convinced that there is a dramatic principle at work may feel that this tale of Sir Thopas comes very suitably from the Pilgrim who was so markedly ready to be impressed at the first sight

---

anoon at once

of his fellow-Pilgrims. But surely the whole point of the situation is the unerring speed and totally deceptive ease with which Chaucer picks up the characterisation handed to him by Harry Bailly—and develops it so effectively that Harry Bailly has to cry quits and the tale of poor Sir Thopas ends in mid-'Fit'. Anything, the Host is certain, would be better than this laboured conformity to 'myrthe'; and so Chaucer is given the right of way—to tell a story in which there is 'som murthe *or* som doctryne' (VII 935), secure in his injured innocence from all further interruptions—'Or elles, certes, ye been to daungerous' (VII 939). Claims for firm relevance between General Prologue characterisation and performance as teller must take heed of *both* performances by Chaucer the Pilgrim; and if one seems to fit very well with the role of naïf and unworldly observer, it is abundantly clear that it is adopted to turn the tables on an over-assured Host— as confident a judge of character as some latter-day readers. (Harry Bailly, however, has to endure the consequences of his mistake, while the modern reader is free to 'Turne over the leef and chese another tale'.) What is implied in the whole characterisation—Chaucer as teller of both *Sir Thopas* and *Melibee*—is not solely the range of his capacity as narrator (sometimes to be the innocent abroad, and some-times the dutiful exponent of 'olde bokes') but his unfailing ability to be one step ahead of the game, to evade the characterisation an audience would, knowingly or not, pin upon their narrator—and, in doing so, cease to attend. Against this typically medieval form of the intentionalist fallacy the only effective device is surprise, a tactical resourcefulness which turns to sound advantage the deference required of an author in the presence of his auditors. As author of *The Canterbury Tales*, Chaucer solves the purely external problem—what sort of story he is to give himself—by taking on two of the least obviously meritorious tales in the whole collection. There is a manifest humour in his having no better and no worse fare to offer than *Sir Thopas* and *Melibee*—the one a comically inadequate little rhyme, the other a solid piece of edifying matter. But there is a less obvious humour in the ease and swiftness with which Harry Bailly is handled and the company landed with 'this litel tretys heere'. If we wish to press

---

to daungerous too hard to please   *chese* choose   *tretys* treatise

questions of dramatic connection, we must not fail to see that what is to be taken into account is the entire performance—phases one and two of Chaucer's little plan: and that what is relevant to its successful execution is not simply the characterisation of Chaucer the Pilgrim, floundering from one half to the other of his disastrously limited repertoire, but the total experience of Chaucer the writer in an oral tradition—opening the range and moving in for the kill as his whole art had trained him to do.

In that context, *Sir Thopas* is a *tour de force:* here is the court's own *joculator* mercilessly parodying the matter and the manner of the market-place entertainer, even to the shout that drowns the hubbub which breaks out when the minstrel must stop to draw breath at the end of a 'Fit'.

> Now holde youre mouth—

the cry rings out: and in the sudden silence the market-place entertainer hastily modulates into the *politesse* of

> —*par charitee,*

an oral equivalent of the restaurant French of later pretensions—for are they not, one and all,

> Both knyght and lady free?

'As performed before all the Crowned Heads of Europe' is the note of this inspired fooling. And what better entertainment for a genuinely sophisticated audience than this view of *le high life?*—a tale that not only parodies the breathless anti-climax of the bob and wheel form—

> Child, by Termagaunt!
> But if thou prike out of myn haunt,
> Anon I sle thy steede
>   With mace—   (VII 810–13)

but also solemnly lists the unknightly accomplishments of the hero while placing him beyond reproach as the epitome of unsullied virtue.

Child! Sir Knight!   *Termagaunt* a heathen idol   *But if* unless   *prike* ride
sle (will) slay

There is a characteristic deflation in store for Sir Thopas. He may lack
a proper training at arms, but he's very handsomely turned out—

> His robe was of syklatoun,
> That coste many a jane.   (VII 734–5)[18]

We may be reminded of that unpromising meeting between a certain
Second Lieutenant Mansfield and his first Adjutant; who, after a long
silence which took in a shirt and tie 'more yellow than khaki' and
breeches 'of a bright buff', exclaimed 'Christ! who's your tailor?'[19]

Only a narrator fully in charge of his material could in swift succession act the roles of market-place *joculator* and the mildly nettled
bookish man who turns with relief to what he knows is good stuff.
To link these two as manifestations of Chaucer the Pilgrim is to risk
flattening the writer's real achievement, by minimising his powers of
improvisation and their distinctive scope in those surprises of characterisation which allow freedom and variety in the choice and conduct
of the Tales.

(V)

The best perspective is surely the simplest—to ask which Tales
touch the heights and thus constitute the standard by which to assess
Chaucer's achievement. For Chaucer's earliest disciples the invocation
with which the Prioress begins her tale would undoubtedly stand high
among the attained felicities of 'aureate' language:

> O mooder Mayde! o mayde Mooder free!
> O bussh unbrent, brennynge in Moyses sighte,
> That ravyshedest doun fro the Deitee,
> Thurgh thyn humblesse, the Goost that in
>   th'alighte,
> Of whos vertu, whan he thyn herte lighte,
> Conceyved was the Fadres sapience,
> Help me to telle it in thy reverence!   (VII 467–73)

---

syklatoun fine scarlet cloth   *jane* (small) coin, 'a good few bob'
mooder mother   *free* noble   *unbrent* unconsumed   *brennynge* burning
That ravyshedest, etc. Thou who through thy humility didst draw down from
the Godhead the Spirit that alighted in thee   *vertu* power   *lighte* illuminated
sapience wisdom (manifest in Christ)

E

Here is achievement indeed. The polysyllables of romance-adoption can give a resounding close ('sapience': 'reverence'); placed at the beginning and end, they constitute the 'springing line' on which the whole arch is projected ('*Conceyved* was the Fadres *sapience*'); or, standing medially (as, 'ravyshedest'), they carry, cantilever-like, the line's weight. In such apposite placing we may see the real attraction of 'aureation' when it is not meaningless embellishment. It stands as the great safeguard against a danger ever-present in a language characterised by dominance of stress and frequency of monosyllable. 'Ten low words' are always ready to do their fatal work.

This highly wrought exordium, with its near-liturgical gravity, leads into a tale of singular simplicity, whose effect is all pathos—but a pathos uncloyed by sentiment. Is this the work of Madame Eglentyne, the unforgettable Prioress of the General Prologue, with her delicately absurd table-manners ('Lyons Corner-house manners', Aldous Huxley once called them), her constant concern 'to countrefete cheere Of court', her quietly indecorous dress, and over all the ambiguity of *Amor vincit omnia?* That portrait has been characterised forever in Lowes's unerring phrase: it reveals the 'delightfully imperfect submergence of the woman in the nun'. But who is the Prioress who tells the tale? Are we to say that her feelings about the boy-martyr show her as a frustrated mother?: that the concern for him is, in these terms, comparable with her excessive care for her troop of pet dogs? We misconceive the General Prologue account if we re-read it in this light. The 'smale houndes' are not surrogate-children: they are substitutes for a great lady's *brachet*; and in feeding them with 'rosted flessh, or milk and wastel-breed' the Prioress is playing the *grande dame*, distributing *largesse* to her retinue. As to the tale itself, critics for whom the pathetic is an inherently absurd mode cannot perhaps be blamed for finding that 'the pathos of her tale is deliberately sentimentalised, particularly through a relentless repetition of certain emotion-producing words, such as "mooder", "child" and "litel"—"This litel child, his litel book lerninge".'[20] Against this, one can only ask the reader to attend to the planned simplicities of the tale, with its frequent

---

countrefete cheere Of court copy aristocratic behaviour   *Amor* etc. Love conquers all   *brachet* hound   *wastel-breed* fine white bread

reminders of an earnest narrator ('As I have seyd', 'I seye that', and, with innocent insistence, 'This hooly monk, this abbot, hym meene I . . .'). Certainly it is a pathetic story: but pathos is not in itself an ignoble aim, and Chaucer makes it not less but more acceptable in coming from a woman religious. The refutation of alleged sentimentality is, I think, this: that when the action of the story has come to its climax, in the entombment of the martyr, there is no rhetorical outburst, no false heroics. There is a prayer to that other boy-martyr, Hugh of Lincoln; and that is all. As to the 'emotion-producing' words, it must not be forgotten that the story is the story of a miracle—and a miracle of the Virgin. The words 'mooder', 'child' and 'litel' keep the perspectives set in the exordium but translate them into homelier and universal terms, so fulfilling the prayer, 'Help me to telle it in thy reverence'. We end, as we began, with invocation of the Virgin: but the course of the story may be measured in the distance travelled from the measured beauty of the appeal at the start to the utter simplicity of the single line with which we end. If we are determined to fit this story into the unforgettable characterisation of the General Prologue we must call into play our modern suspicions (suspicions which have their own foundation, but that is another matter) and view dourly any essay in that commonest of medieval modes, the pathetic—even if we stop short of Mr Spearing's discovery of 'a self-indulgent pleasure in the emotions aroused by brutality juxtaposed with innocence'. The trouble is that to support any such line we must not only do some redoubtable arguing from silence. What is worse, we shall read limiting and even disabling overtones into a story of great simplicity. The plain function of the Prioress's Tale, its conception and placing at this point, is surely clear. We are dealing with an integral section of the Tales. After the neat sophistication and the naked appetites of the Shipman's Tale, a serious story is called for if the balance is to be held firm. Seriousness to a medieval audience means, inevitably, pathos, stories of hapless sufferers. Into Chaucer's mind may well have come the story of young Hugh of Lincoln, through Philippa's being included in a memorandum of admission to the fraternity of Lincoln Cathedral (1386).[21] Who would be an appropriate teller of a tale about a boy-martyr? None better than a woman religious; and so Chaucer makes his Host turn with notable courtesy to a Prioress.

But, in a very real sense, if we are to hold to dramatic relevance, we do not have *a* Prioress: we have Lady Sweetbriar, *bele Eglentine*. Once again, if we are to attend to the tale, we must not be over-concerned about the teller characterised in the General Prologue.

It is better, in fact, if we are to get things in the right proportion, to stand the argument on its head, asking first which are the best tales and then seeing what degree of dramatic relevance there is in them. By common consent a high place must go to the Nun's Priest's Tale and the Franklin's Tale. Here are wonderfully intricate examples of narrative art, the more so for being held in a gently ironic perspective. The Nun's Priest's 'tale is of a cok, as ye may heere' (VII 3252). So we might, if only the narrator could keep to the point. All men (none more readily than the 'patristic' critics of modern times) can see that the story of 'Chauntecleer the faire' and his enemy 'daun Russell the fox' is so handled that mighty issues peep through—the significance of dreams and the question of free-will versus predestination, foremost among them. But we may also see, if we care to look, that in the very human foreground there is at work a wholly satisfactory kind of even-handed justice. The cock may be conceited enough to think authoritative teaching too subtle for his wife. But her simple-minded determinism—all dreams are *insomnia*,[22] and there's an end of it—is in fact mistaken. Flattery leads to the downfall of the cock: but the fox is subject to it, too. All the learning deployed in the *ambiance* of the story serves as focus to the human drama. If you keep your head there is always a chance: men can learn from experience—at least not to make the same mistake twice. These are the clear issues of the story proper. We are free to make what we can of the mighty matters that encompass mortal choice. Of course, the audience must not be supposed to think a simple story worth their attention. The narrator, much like Chauntecleer in the moment of release, in his turn flies upward—

> Taketh the moralite, goode men!

All is written for our doctrine, so

> Taketh the fruyt, and lat the chaf be stille.   (VII 3440, 3444)

---

cok cock   *daun* Master   *insomnia* non-veridical dreams   *moralite* moral (of the story)

We must not undo the narrator's work, taking him *au pied de la lettre* and industriously transposing background and foreground. As Donaldson has acutely remarked of such laborious misunderstanding, 'the fruit' of this tale 'is its chaff'.[23] Least of all may we persist with the question, who is this narrator? We do not know him from any General Prologue portrait. He springs into life at Harry Bailly's bidding, one more victim of the Host's jocular condescension towards the dim and scholarly: and, surprisingly, one more who acquits himself in the holiday task of telling 'a murie tale'.

Almost its opposite in conception is the Franklin's Tale. If the Nun's Priest tells from his resources of learning a tale that returns his audience to the unmistakable realities of life, the Franklin approaches his tale with a determined preconception in favour of a code of behaviour only to be found in notably rare spirits, those who are 'gentil',[24] and he ends on a plane where love is triumphantly immune to all tests. Where the Nun's Priest rides forward out of obscurity, the Franklin is carefully established in 'the wordes of the Frankeleyn to the Squier, and the wordes of the Hoost to the Frankeleyn'. Towards the Squire the Franklin has nothing but admiration:

> thow hast thee wel yquit
> And *gentilly* . . .   (V 673–4)

We may perhaps take it as the most skilful interruption so far; but its cause is not far to seek. In the Squire the Franklin sees a mirror of the might-have-been, the graces lacking in his own son whose concern is only with feckless misspending, so that

> he hath levere talken with a page
> Than to comune with any *gentil* wight
> Wher he myghte lerne *gentillesse* aright.   (V 697–8)

This is too much for Harry Bailly, who fears for the succession of tales if we are to be held up by reminiscent sententiousness:

> 'Straw for youre *gentillesse*!' quod oure Hoost—

and he brings the Franklin, as he thinks, down to earth by reminding

---

thee . . . yquit acquitted yourself   *levere* rather   *comune with* converse with

him of the agreement and by conveying that reminder with the 'thou'
of emphatic directness—'pardee, sire, wel *thou* woost'. But the
Franklin is not put out: his reply is in formal and ceremonious terms

> That knowe I wel, *sire* . . .
> I prey *yow*, haveth me nat in desdeyn . . .   (V 699–700)

and he continues in this markedly polite vein even after the curt
injunction, 'Telle on thy tale withouten wordes mo',

> 'Gladly, sire Hoost,' quod he, 'I wole obeye
> Unto your wyl: now herkneth what I seye.
> I wol yow nat contrarien in no wyse
> As fer as that my wittes wol suffyse.
> I prey to God that it may plesen yow;
> Thanne woot I wel that it is good ynow.'   (V 703–8)

This ceremonious deference brings into relief a Pilgrim who, unlike
some others, will not rebel against the Host's leading even when it is
abrupt to the point of discourtesy. 'Gentillesse', it appears, is not a
remote and cloistered virtue:[25] and 'gentillesse' is firmly underlined
as he moves into his prologue:

> Thise olde *gentil* Britouns in hir dayes . . .   (V 709)

It is an older man, one who views the present generation critically,
who speaks. The virtue he celebrates is placed in far-off time; and it
is moved a little farther from actuality when the speaker apologises for
his inadequacy. He is a homespun character ('burel man') and knows
nothing of rhetorical art. Indeed, his grasp of the terminology is
somewhat shaky, if enough to make the obvious joke:

> Colours ne knowe I none, withouten drede,
> But swich colours as growen in the mede,
> Or elles swich as men dye or peynte.   (V 723–5)

This unpolished but quietly enthusiastic advocate of fine behaviour is
a narrator whom Chaucer deploys with great skill. The detail of the

---

woost knowest   *contrarien* oppose, thwart   *ynow* enough   *Britouns* Bretons,
inhabitants of Brittany   *Colours* rhetorical devices   *withouten drede* without
doubt   *mede* field

story will concern us later. What we should notice now is that Chaucer
has led from the Squire's spirited but somewhat inept performance to
the uncritical admiration of one who, seeing the social graces, sees a
world of desire fulfilled. The older man who contentedly tells a story
of life as ideally noble people live it is a figure touched with gentle
ridicule. High life seen from the outside is the distinctive focus of the
story, and as such it holds particular amusement for a courtly narrator.
We have seen Harry Bailly relentlessly bent on 'swich thyng as may
oure hertes glade'. He is the plain man who will level all into remorseless
bonhomie. There is one face of unsophistication, life outside 'society'.
But the Franklin puts him down with ease; and in the Franklin we
see the other face of innocence—a face like that of the 'turtle trewe'
who in *The Parliament of Fowls* had enthusiastically espoused the
cause of the 'gentils'. In the Franklin of end-link and prologue we meet
a settled depth of uncritical idealism.

Can we link this Franklin unequivocally with the Franklin of the
General Prologue? There we have the portrait of a man whose place
in the social order is variable, but is below the 'gentil' as it is firmly
above the churl.[26] He is the man of conscious merit, one who has
arrived at a proper station in life; and like most such he is open-handed
with creature-comforts, for he assumes that they at least constitute one
standard which all men must acknowledge. The concern that everything
should be of an unvaryingly good standard ('alweys after oon', I 341)
is of a piece with the testiness towards any inefficiency. No lapse can
be contemplated:

> Wo was his cook but if his sauce were
> Poynaunt and sharp, and redy al his geere.   (I 351–2)

Can we connect 'Epicurus owene sone' with the Franklin who dotes
on 'gentillesse'? Certainly, when we come to the Tale there is a familiar
note in the fullness of the magician's household provision:

> Hem lakked no vitaille that myghte hem plese.
> So wel arrayed hous as ther was oon
> Aurelius in his lyf saugh nevere noon: (V 1186–8)

Poynaunt piquant   *geere* equipment   *vitaille* food, 'provisions'

and there is a revealing peremptoriness in the magician's treatment of
his squire:

> Is redy oure soper?
> Almost an houre it is, I undertake,
> Sith I yow bad oure soper for to make . . .   (V 1210–12)

Here, too, an efficiently-run household is proof against all tests:

> 'Sire,' quod this squier, 'whan it liketh yow,
> It is al redy, though ye wol right now.'   (V 1215–16)

All this will, inevitably, stir memories of the Franklin of the General
Prologue, and there is no great harm in our linking the two if we must
—as long as we recognise the real difference between them, and not
blur it by talking loosely of an advance or deepening in a constant
characterisation. We are very ready to obey that greatest of modern
imperatives, 'Only connect'. But we must not assume that Chaucer or
his audience felt the same impulse or were troubled by similar criteria
of verisimilitude or even plain consistency. Our impulse to make
working connections—to supply or 'understand' links which Chaucer
has not in fact given—is no doubt the characteristic of our time. As
such, it is strictly comparable with what we very readily deride in
other ages—in the seventeenth and eighteenth centuries, the unceasing
itch to rewrite him, or, in the later nineteenth and the twentieth
centuries, the urge to defend him against the damning charge of
lacking 'high seriousness' (by which, as Chesterton once remarked,
was usually meant high and dry solemnity). But in all these instances,
admiration conceals tyranny. If we will have the author do what we
are determined to praise him for, then what he has in fact done may
escape our notice.

   In the present instance the characterisation in end-link and individual
prologue shapes the Franklin-narrator to be an observer of idealised life.
Given that, it is entirely appropriate that he should see shrewdly into
the wordly briskness of the magician; as it is appropriate that the
gentlefolk of his story, who start at a declared remove from the
common run, should, as the story moves on, enjoy the Franklin's

---

soper supper   *undertake* declare

protection from the world of getting and spending. The Franklin-narrator is one who mediates between a world he knows and one which remains forever beyond the possibility of his knowing:

> Who koude telle, but he hadde wedded be,
> The joy, the ese, and the prosperitee . . . ?   (V 803–4)

It is, no doubt, a thrust that harks back to the Merchant's declared unhappiness (IV 1213 ff.). But the narrator's overriding achievement is to keep the happiness of Dorigen and Arveragus at a safe remove from over-intent scrutiny. So, when separation comes, it is fitting that Dorigen should lament:

> wepeth she and siketh,
> As doon *thise noble wyves whan hem liketh*—   (V 817–8)

But there can be no intrusion upon her grief. The Franklin is left hastily crowding on the merely generalised detail—

> She moorneth, waketh, wayleth, fasteth, pleyneth.   (V 819)

If we are to press for congruity with the Franklin of the General Prologue, we can say no more than 'not wholly inappropriate'. But should we not ask whether the whole impulse to link the narrator with the Pilgrim characterised in the General Prologue, and to see the characterisation as extended and deepened in the end-link and narrator's prologue, is of any real utility? The gains, on any showing, are minimal, amounting to no more than a superficial claim for Chaucer as first (if in a crude and sometimes halting way) in a procession of naturalistic novelists and dramatists—one obligingly ready, 'upon occasion', to sacrifice 'absolute literary criteria' (whatever that may mean) 'in favour of dramatic decorum'.[27] Such claims, of course, must be eked out with encouragement to tolerate those features the modern reader may rate as deficiencies, and varied by browbeating assertion of connections that he might, unaided, totally miss. The author who emerges is a suitable candidate for inclusion in a House of Fame which Chaucer himself might have had difficulty in recognising —a master of *bonhomie* which, all-pervading, is the distinctive light

---

but he unless he   *siketh* sighs   *waketh* lies sleepless   *pleyneth* laments

in which his works are to be read. More important, if we insist upon the sheer identity of the General Prologue Franklin and the narrator of the tale we are hardly likely to detect the delicate pattern Chaucer develops with a narrator who, much like himself on other occasions, starts at a safe remove from the story, only to find himself enamoured of his heroine. But this time the narrator, more fortunate than Chaucer himself, can bring all to a happy ending, when crucial tests are triumphantly survived.

(VI)

If then we ask what are *The Canterbury Tales*, if they are not essentially dramatic, revelations of character in action, the answer is they are *tales*. The principle of variety is all-important, and to attain that variety—to deversify *fabliau* with *tragedye*, uncompromising homily with tail-rime romance, beast-fable with epic, saint's legend with Breton lay—to achieve this 'plenty', Chaucer skilfully, through accepted type-casting as well as unexpected turns of situation, creates openings and establishes the ground of retaliation, moves up his hitherto anonymous figures as opportunities open for them, heads off the expected, effecting real surprise, and in general shepherds his Pilgrim company along their way. His surrogate is Harry Bailly—whose failures in judgment are matched, appropriately to holiday time, with his plain man's contempt for anything that is not outright 'mirth' or 'solas'. We do not know at what stage in the general period of composition of the Tales Chaucer wrote his General Prologue. The story of Saint Cecilia (which became the Second Nun's Tale), and the tragedies later allotted to the Monk, can be placed after *The House of Fame* and before *The Parliament of Fowls*, with *Palamon* (subsequently developed into the Knight's Tale) coming between the *Parliament* and *Troilus and Criseyde*. These earlier pieces, as we have seen, have only a moderate degree of connection with their tellers or (as with the Monk) come with an effect of surprise. Of tales later in date, only two (making notable use of autobiographical prologue) unarguably complement and extend what was said of their narrators in the General

solas entertainment, relief

Prologue; they are the tales of Wife of Bath and Pardoner, rascals both. For the rest, we are not to assume a large area of unfulfilled intention, attributable to the Tales being unfinished at Chaucer's death. Rather, we must look more closely at the relation of tale and teller in the story itself and (often) in end-link and prologue to that story. Above all, we should attend to the larger principle of contrast within the collection taken as a whole—the clash of contraries affording an illustration of life as we know it, in which piety and obscenity, knockabout farce and solemn submission to Destiny, exist not so much in mutual opposition as in general and cumulative testimony to man's many-sided nature. It is the nearest thing we have to a genuinely free creation—not least because it is unfinished. Dryden's phrase 'God's plenty' may be pressed; for this, too, is a plenty initiated and sustained by a continuing act of benevolence. Chaucer's greatest achievement is to *create*, in the only sense that matters. His creatures are free; and the mark of his delight in their freedom is that when the author visits his own creation he does so in unfeigned humility and entire goodwill.

6

AUCTORITEE AND PREF

The Canterbury Tales (II)

Is there any one formative principle at work in the whole collection of Canterbury Tales? Nearly sixty years ago the existence of a 'Marriage Group' was propounded: that is, that with the Third Section or Group D there begins a series of seven tales dealing (though interruptedly) with 'a single subject or topic, the seat and conduct of authority in married life'.[1] In this view the sequence would begin with the Wife of Bath arguing for the *maistrie* of wife over husband. After the first interruption (the paired animosities of Friar and Summoner) the Clerk takes the contrary line, as a good clerk should, showing Griselda as the perfect example of wifely submissiveness. In the Merchant's Tale we are back to female sovereignty once more: the old man January is deceived by his young wife, May. The Squire's unfinished tale is treated as a second interruption, since it does not bear directly on the theme of the balance of power in marriage; and with the Franklin's Tale the sequence is brought to a conclusion. 'Love wol nat been constreyned by maistrye'. Dorigen and Arveragus exemplify an ideal relationship. He is 'Servant in love and lord in marriage'; and this relationship, standing firm, leads to a happy deliverance from impending disaster.

(I)

We may first of all qualify this account slightly by pointing out that the debate is essentially a holiday one. The Wife of Bath, as we have seen earlier, is the licensed Fool of the company: she represents that characteristically medieval taste which sees true comedy in strict inversion of truth. Medieval canonists might debate how much correction was due to a wife from her husband. The comic solution is exactly to invert the problem: let the wife beat the husband. Accordingly, we are not to take the debate *au grand sérieux*. The Friar, as we have seen, had ironically pointed out that great matters were involved in the Wife's discussion. 'Dame', he begins with mock deference

> Ye han heer touched, also moot I thee,
> In scole-matere greet difficultee—   (III 1271–2)

but he had more pressing concerns in hand. The Clerk is the appropriate one to take up the 'auctoritees' which the Friar sets aside in favour of more obvious 'game':

> But, dame, heere as we ryde by the weye,
> Us nedeth nat to speken but of game,
> And lete auctoritees, on Goddes name,
> To prechyng and to scole eek of clergye.   (III 1274–7)

When the Clerk's turn comes, he acquits himself very creditably— by retracting his obvious moral in an *Envoi* which sets a pattern of submission to the Wife of Bath's holiday authority. This pattern is amusingly kept alive. The Merchant refers to her by name, as an authority on marriage. His own tale is savagely realistic. On his way to the *pref* of a sordid deception, January listens to varying views:

> Diverse men diversely hym tolde
> Of mariage manye ensamples olde.
> Somme blamed it, somme preysed it, certeyn . . .   (IV 1469–71)

But one question does not arise. There is no need to ask how can he expect the joys of heaven if he is happy in marriage. The question, says his Brother Justin, is unreal:

---

also moot I thee bless my soul!   *In scole-matere greet difficultee* very tricky scholastic questions   *game* sport, jest   *To prechyng and to scole eek of clergye* for the learned to sermonise and dispute about

> The Wyf of Bathe, *if ye han understonde,*
> Of mariage, which we have on honde,
> Declared hath ful wel in litel space.   (IV 1685–7)

There's no adding to *her* account of the joys of wedded life. Similarly, it is fair to assume that Harry Bailly's glance rests darkly on her when, contributing his grain to the store of practical wisdom, he admits to being ill-matched in marriage—but he will say no more:

> cause why, it sholde reported be
> And toold to hire of somme of this meynee—
> Of whom, it nedeth nat for to declare . . .

Yet he gives a clue, none the less—

> Syn wommen konnen outen swich chaffare,   (IV 2435–8)

a plain echo of the Wife's proclaimed tactic

> With daunger oute we al oure chaffare.   (III 521)

   The debate, then, is a holiday affair; and we must go on to observe that there is wide variation in the 'issues' raised by subsequent speakers. What the Wife of Bath has done—as the Friar is quick to note—is to set in motion a conflict between *auctoritee* and *experience*. That the Clerk should reply is itself a sort of professional rivalry—an improvised type-casting that in its own way answers to the settled antagonism of Friar and Summoner but provides a higher form of 'game'. The Clerk sets forth—with proper length and diffuseness—the virtue of Griselda, and makes his retraction. There is the paired rivalry of *pref* and *auctoritee* at the end of Round One. When the Merchant makes his contribution it is, brutally, from the standpoint of experience; and now there is no discussion of *maistrie* but a bitter portrayal of inevitable deception and defeat. If a husband reports what he sees, then he is told

> Ye han som glymsyng, and no parfit sighte,   (IV 2383)

---

understonde understood   *on honde* (the topic) in hand   *hire* her (Harry Bailly's wife)   *of* by   *meyne* company   *Syn* since   *konnen* know how to, are expert in   *outen* setting out, bringing into the open   *chaffare* wares, matters   *With daunger* etc. We are very coy about spreading out all we have to sell   *glymsyng* fleeting (and therefore unreliable) vision   *parfit* perfect

and he must thankfully accept the lie:

> This Januarie, who is glad but he?   (IV 2412)

The Franklin's Tale is least of all susceptible to the approach that it constitutes a 'solution' to the problem of *soveraynetee*; for here the high relation of Dorigen and Arveragus is the condition on which we have the tale at all. Nothing leads to it; everything proceeds from it. Certainly, the Franklin glances at earlier debate as he introduces his account of this exalted relationship:

> pryvely she fil of his accord
> To take hym for hir housbonde and hir lord,
> *Of swich lordshipe as men han over hir wyves.*   (V 741–3)

But there is no question where his tale is unswervingly directed— towards the vindication of *gentillesse*, and from the standpoint of innocent *auctoritee*. The Franklin reports upon what he is certain must be true—though not alas! in his own experience. The more reason for him to dwell upon the detail of this highly unusual agree- ment. It is entered into, on Arveragus's side, with solemn contractual force:

> Of his free wyl he swoor hire as a knyght
> That nevere in al his lyf he, day ne nyght,
> Ne sholde upon hym tak no maistrie
> Agayn her wyl...   (V 745–8)

and, on Dorigen's side, with a formal courtesy that is itself the expres- sion of *gentillesse*:

> She thanked hym, and with ful greet humblesse
> She seyde, 'Sire, sith of *youre* gentillesse
> *Ye* profre me to have so large a reyne,'   (V 753–5)

where the ceremonious plural both marks the solemnity of her under- taking and augurs well for its fulfilment. Being well aware of what the

---

pryvely privately, tacitly   *fil of his acord* came to agreement with him
Of swich lordshipe as ... in terms of that authority which ...   *profre* offer
large a reyne free a rein, scope

Wife of Bath has said about the state of marriage and the things women
desire, the Franklin now digresses. Before launching upon the story
proper he must enlarge upon the essential point, that free consent
underlies the agreement:

> Love wol nat been constreyned by maistrye . . .
> Love is a thyng as any spirit free.
> Wommen, of kynde, desiren libertee,
> And nat to been constreyned as a thral.   (V 764, 767–9)

Here is a narrator who is determined to assert control, not so much
upon the story as upon his audience. He does this skilfully, drawing
upon what the audience has already experienced. Patience is the
Franklin's theme; in this he takes a leaf from the Clerk's authoritative
books. He can speak from experience, too; and in this he can follow
the Merchant. But this time authority and experience admit no conflict.
We may freely choose to obey established doctrine—or we shall find
ourselves compelled to acknowledge it:

> Lerneth to suffre, or elles, so moot I goon,
> Ye shul it lerne, wher so ye wole or noon.   (V 777–8)

This time, too, experience brings not bitterness but geniality. In the
long range in which the story is already being cast human beings are
readily seen as fallible:

> in this world, certein, ther no wight is
> That he ne dooth or seith somtyme amys.   (V 779–80)

So when the audience is returned to the married pair, it is with a taste
of dramatic irony:

> she to hym ful wisly gan to swere
> That nevere sholde ther be defaute in here.   (V 789–90)

   In this light, there can be no question that the Franklin has been an
attentive listener to what his fellow-pilgrims have said—as in the

---

of kynde by (their) nature   *constreyned* restricted   *thral* slave   *so moot I
goon* I promise you!   *Ye shul it lerne* you'll have to learn it   *wher* whether
ful wisly with great assurance   *defaute* failure (to keep her side of the
agreement)

reference to those who, like the Merchant, are jaundiced by their experience in marriage (V 803-6). Perhaps, too, it is the Squire's would-be harrowing account of the falcon's lament (V 412 ff.) which suggests the comment on Dorigen's sorrow at separation:

> wepeth she and siketh,
> As doon thise noble wyves whan hem liketh.   (V 817-18)

If so, as I have earlier suggested, the Franklin turns it to good advantage: there is no invasion of his heroine's privacy. Perhaps, too, the matter of magical 'apparences' (V 1139 ff.) is another echo of the Squire (V 217-19): undoubtedly 'thise stories' on which the Franklin draws for Dorigen's instances of virtuous women (V 1367 ff.) are all from the treatise which the Wife of Bath's fifth husband liked to read at night: and certainly the Franklin comes to his conclusion with a triumphant emphasis on *gentil* and *gentillesse*, the original point carried against Harry Bailly's rumbling dissent. Perhaps, too, as one editor suggests, the Franklin's tale redeems the types of knight and squire and clerk and squire vilified or satirically presented in, respectively, the Merchant's Tale and the Miller's Tale.[2] Given all this, the Franklin undoubtedly stands at a certain point of cumulative force, in a section of *The Canterbury Tales* which may have had its final arrangement at Chaucer's hands. But what he does not do is offer a solution to any debate on *maistrie*. His is the voice of experience in all matters except that of the high relationship of his wedded aristocrats. They remain beyond his experience, though never out of reach of his benevolence. In that sense, *auctoritee* has the last word in the debate which the Wife of Bath had initiated with her sweeping claim for the self-sufficiency of *experience*. But in what matters most there is common ground. Alice had contended from experience for a practical definition of *gentillesse*:

> ... he is gentil that dooth gentil dedis   (III 1170)

> Looke who that is moost vertuous alway,
> Pryvee and apert, and moost entendeth ay
> To do the gentil dedes that he kan;
> Taak hym for the grettest gentil man.   (III 1113-16)

---

siketh sighs   *Looke who* whoever   *Pryvee and apert* privately and publicly
entendeth purposes   *ay* continually   *that he kan* that lie within his compass

F

The Franklin would not disagree. His wedded pair may be loftily idealised; but their influence is enough to set to rights the world of getting and spending, so that each in turn competes in generosity towards his neighbour:

> Which was the mooste fre, as thynketh yow?   (V 1622)

Here, in the end of the debate, is a story which unites the worlds of *auctoritee* and *experience*.

(II)

In a brief survey of the kind attempted in this and the preceding chapter, scant justice can be done to the fullness of Chaucer's achievement in any one of the Tales. It may go some way to redress the balance if, in conclusion, we examine the Franklin's Tale in some detail, taking it as peculiarly representative of Chaucer's mature art. That art is essentially an art of narration, vividly alert to the susceptibilities of a small audience rather than a solitary reader and endlessly fertile in unobtrusive expedients to control that audience's attention.

The Franklin, as we have seen, stands at a point of cumulative significance within his group of stories. We may think him a Pilgrim especially dear to Chaucer. Certainly, he has held offices which the poet had occupied:[3] but, more important, his standpoint as narrator is the one Chaucer had so often taken. As Chaucer throughout his career stood (or liked to represent himself as standing) to his courtly audience—simple-minded, fond of old things, decently diffident in putting his views but not shirking honest 'sentence' on occasion—so the Franklin now stands. But this time the story has a happy ending: initial confidence in the old stories is not misplaced; what is noble and necessary in an aristocratic pair of lovers turns out to be perfectly possible for others in their turn; and, given this high example, all issues in an entire naturalness of behaviour, best felt in the affable condescension with which a professional magician dismisses his crestfallen debtor:

> Sire, I releesse thee thy thousand pound,
> As thou right now were cropen out of the ground!   (V 1613–14)

---

fre noble, magnanimous, disinterested   *As* as if   *were cropen out* had crept out

The Franklin, clearly, is a more fortunate narrator than the learned author of the *tragedye* of *Troilus and Criseyde*, venturing in his own person on a story of high-minded innocence which, isolated in an unrepentantly real world, came all to grief. We may see this transformation from another standpoint by comparing the Franklin's with the Shipman's Tale. There, too, are a married pair and a would-be intruder; a bargain; and a sum of money. But there the ending of the story is to ask how shall I score off my neighbour? Here the tumble-home is to ask how can I defer to the interest of others? The persons of the Franklin's Tale bow each other out, and we are left with the triumphant question, 'Which was the mooste fre?' The success of the tale is precisely to make the question unanswerable. Not many readers, one supposes, would think that the story held out a definitive answer to him who could unravel it.[4] Contrariwise, in the Shipman's Tale, there is no question who gets off best. The two tales are diptych-like: the same essential situation and virtually the same mechanism works to wholly different ends. In the width of understanding this presupposes we may see Chaucer's working range, and consequently be dislodged from any easy identification of the poet himself—so that the whole achievement itself constitutes a sort of *demande*, as George Kane acutely notes.[5]

The mature work of the Franklin's Tale raises some problems for modern criticism which are relatively constant in Chaucer's development—most notably, that mixture of comic and serious effects which sometimes leaves the modern reader uncertain of the preponderant effect in any one instance. C. S. Lewis was not the first (and is not likely to be the last) to reprove 'comic effects' in *The Book of the Duchess* which he found 'disastrous and ... certainly not intended'.[6] The Franklin is clearly to some extent comic. The hard questions are how far? and upon what occasions? In what follows I take some leading instances: first, Dorigen's celebrated questioning of the ways of Providence (V 865–94).

This begins on a manifestly solemn note, the model exordium 'O stelliferi conditor orbis':

O stelliferi etc. Creator of the starry heaven (Boeth. I, m. 5)

> Eterne God, that thurgh thy purveiaunce
> Ledest the world by certein governaunce . . .

It is such a beginning as we might expect of the Franklin, with his modest store of rhetorical knowledge and his sense of the fitness of the occasion. But where is he to go from there?—straight down to homely protest:

> But, Lord, thise grisly feendly rokkes blake . . .

and to the honest objection that they

> semen rather a foul confusion
> Of werk than any fair creacion
> Of swich a parfit wys God and a stable—

all of which leads to the plain question

> Why han ye wroght this werk unresonable?

There is no middle ground for this narrator between 'heigh style' and plain speaking; just as there is no subtlety in formal argument. His character knows there are proofs of Divine benevolence—plenty of them:

> I woot wel clerkes wol seyn as hem leste,
> By argumentz, that al is for the beste.

But there is only one 'conclusion' anyone can truly reach: to hope for the best—

> As kepe my lord! this my conclusion.
> To clerkes lete I al disputison.

With that, heartfelt simplicity returns and the tempo quickens:

> But wolde God that alle thise rokkes blake
> Were sonken into helle for his sake!
> Thise rokkes sleen myn herte for the feere:

and the rest is left not so much to our imagination as to our sympathy.

---

purveiaunce providence, (wise) provision   *certein* sure   *feendly* hostile, menacing   *foul* ugly   *stable* constant, unchanging   *unresonable* unjustifiable, excessive   *clerkes* the learned   *As kepe* may (God) keep   *sleen* slay, destroy

The scene ends with the character still in the act of lament:

> Thus wolde she seyn, with many a pitous teere.

The extent to which the narrator is technically unskilled—in not having varied and subtle resources with which to handle the matter— is the extent to which we become convinced of his heroine's independent existence. If no resource of language or argument can amplify or modulate her doubt and grief, then that grief becomes not less but more real—provided only that the narrator does not attempt to cover his deficiencies. That is why the end of the episode is so important. The Franklin puts her back into her story, on which we have for a moment intruded. The independence of character and narrator is, so to speak, guaranteed in Dorigen's continuing misery:

> Thus wolde she seyn, with many a pitous teere.

The technique is much the same when we come to a second notable instance, her 'compleynt' against Fortune (V 1355–1456). The Franklin starts 'with ful devout corage' on the vast store of *exempla* that will fortify Dorigen in her choice of death before dishonour. But by line 1377 a certain briskness is apparent, as though consciousness of the weight of *exempla* yet to be told requires a greater neatness of despatch—

> They prively been *stirt* into a welle,
> And dreynte hemselven, as the bookes telle

(it's all there in the record, if anyone wants to go into detail). The same speeding-up is evident at line 1402—an obliging alacrity in self-immolation:

> She took her children alle, and *skipte adoun*
> Into the fyr . . .

The Franklin's mode of ending this episode is the same as before. The debate continues, *exempla* can still be marshalled—

> The same thyng I seye of Bilyea,
> Of Rodogone, and eek Valeria—

---

prively secretly   *been stirt* have jumped   *dreynte* drowned

but the last light falls on Dorigen at her hopeless task:

> Thus pleyned Dorigen a day or tweye,
> Purposynge evere that she wolde deye.

How much of this comes with an intended humour? For a courtly audience, no doubt, there is a gleam of amusement in a well-intentioned narrator's desire to do well by his heroine in her status as tragedy queen. But this does not undercut the pathos of the situation: if the narrator cannot help, who can? It is for this reason that we should be on our guard against critics who ridicule or belittle Dorigen. We must not, for example, misconceive those lines in which, addressing Providence, she refuses to itemise victims of the cruel rocks—

> An hundred thousand bodyes of mankynde
> Han rokkes slayn, *al be they nat in mynde* ...

The phrase springs from the narrator's inadequacy. But it is an inadequacy in the facile or glib, and as such it allows no escape from the reality of impatient anxiety. It is the same when Dorigen openly takes Providence to task:

> Why han ye wroght this werk unresonable?
> For by this werk, south, north, ne west, ne eest,
> Ther nys yfostred man, ne bryd, ne beest;
> *It dooth no good, to my wit, but anoyeth.*

Critics have not been slow to pounce upon this as evidence of Dorigen's shallowness. She is willing to believe, they say, in omnipotent benevolence; but perhaps it needs a cautionary word now and again. All, she agrees, is for the best, and scholars can prove it—at least to their satisfaction; only, please don't let Arveragus suffer. Certainly the characterisation is clear enough in these terms. But what is equally clear is that the Franklin, too, wants a happy issue for Dorigen and Arveragus. He, too, is unable either to argue the case, or to phrase her distress in any more exalted terms. Just as with the later 'compleynt'

---

evere continually   *deye* die   *unresonable* unjustifiable, unfair   *yfostred* fed [the rocks are barren]   *bryd* bird   *to my wit* as I see it   *anoyeth* does (real) harm

The Franklin, then, is not all amiable incompetence. Chaucer's [pri]mary skill is to make him pity what he cannot approve, and state [sim]ply what he is unable to elaborate. This is the counterpart of [bu]siness-like ease and despatch when it is a matter of things within the [nar]rator's ken. We have earlier seen him briskly characterising the [pro]fessional magician, dwelling on the skill with which that practised [ma]n of affairs gives his audience a preview of his powers, and then [wit]h apparent abruptness breaks off for supper (V 1189–1218). The [sam]e agreeable competence is evident in the Franklin's handling of the [tra]nsitions of his tale—as,

> Lete I this woful creature lye;
> Chese he, for me, wheither he wol lyve or dye—   (V 1085–6)

> But thus they mette, of aventure or grace—   (V 1508)

[wh]ere the audience may please themselves what significance they attach [to] details which are not plainly essential to the onward drive of the [sto]ry. This practice of understatement has something of the impact [of] what in the theatre is called throw-away technique. It marks the [kin]d and degree of the narrator's absorption in his story, and as such [h]elps to strengthen our belief in that story as something existing [ind]ependently of the present narrator and, by implication, capable of [oth]er handling, including our own. This indifference to certain kinds [of] effect is complemented by a firm grasp on what the narrator *does* [thin]k relevant, and this is above all evident in the sharpness of the [sto]ry's incidental detail, so increasing the effect of honest reporting. [For] example, Aurelius in company with his lady—

> It may wel be he looked on hir face
> In swich a wise as man that asketh grace;
> But nothyng wiste she of his entente.   (V 957–9)

[Th]e same laconic note is heard when Arveragus returns:

> No thyng list hym to been ymaginatyf—   (V 1094)

[Ches]e he let him choose *for me* for all I care *of aventure or grace* whether [by c]hance or providentially *nothing wiste she* she had no idea *No thyng* [list h]ym, etc. he had no cause to be suspicious

(lines 1355–1456), his heart isn't in it. There is an anticipatory spirit of optimism in him. If it is culpable to want those you love exempted from the hazards which even Benevolence itself has contrived, then he is the first offender.

Chaucer has cast the Franklin well for this role of genial narrator, one whose susceptibilities to the exalted status of his characters will be fortified by natural optimism. Chaucer himself, as narrator of the 'double sorwes' of Troilus, was fluent, versatile in language, knowledgeable in the extreme. There was no lack of skill either in the beautifully turned proems, or in the delicate embroideries of his 'medievalisation' of the story; and no lack of learning in the major digressions—upon Fortune, Free-Will, planetary conjunction, and the like. When the narrator of the *tragedye* can go no farther, it is not through any deficiency in his equipment. Consequently, there can be no turning away from the books, no possibility of enlisting sympathy for characters who have been misrepresented. On the contrary, the books are to be searched for those mitigating circumstances which the responsible author cannot invent: 'Take every man now to his bokes heede'. The break-out into happiness comes only by escape from the story. The author had put on a decorous sadness ('to a sorwful tale, a sory chere'); but he could not anticipate the emptiness with which he must finally quit a story grown too painful in the telling. Contrariwise, can a narrator who is predisposed in favour of happiness—one who is determined to find in his two lovers the shining vindication of *gentillesse*—hope to fare any better? A good part of the answer lies in a certain genial incapacity on the Franklin's part. It is this which keeps the story at a distinct remove from him; and in this he is sharply different from the author of *Troilus and Criseyde*, a narrator who was admirably qualified to prepare each successive step, to report with the utmost fidelity, and where necessary to head off misunderstanding—qualified, too, to share a growing sense of foreboding, and to read the portents even while continuing to hope. With the Franklin things are quite the reverse. He will do his willing but limited best ('I shal seyn with good wyl as I kan'); and as for prophetic insights—well, try as he may to be the philosopher, cheerfulness will keep breaking in.

(III)

The characterisation of the Franklin-narrator is skilfully developed from his initial casting as being no hand at 'rethorik':

> Thyng that I speke, it moot be bare and pleyn.

Since this at once goes on to a rhetorical apology—

> I sleep nevere on the Mount of Pernaso,
> Ne lerned Marcus Tullius Scithero—   (V 720–2)

we are attuned to the technique of an initial stab at the appropriate language, followed by a side-slip into blatant simplicity—as in the famous instance:

> Th'orisonte hath reft the sonne his lyght—
> This is as much to seye as it was nyght!   (V 1017–18)[7]

This helps to give the audience purchase upon the story. Free from the obligation to attend to an omnicompetent guide, we at once respond to this unprofessional narrator's enthusiasm—and his wish to get on with the story. If we want something more elaborately finished then, no help for it, we must supply it ourselves. This is, of course, Chaucer's moment of opportunity and he exploits it brilliantly. In the story which the Franklin is partly telling, partly obscuring, at this moment the sun is going down: and with it goes exalted language, for this is a moment when the ways begin to part. Irrevocably, it seems, some are happy, some miserable:

> hoom they goon in joye and in solas,
> Save oonly wrecche Aurelius, allas!   (V 1019–20)

The Franklin has only stock epithets: but 'joye' and 'solas' answer soundly to the expectable happiness of aristocratic leisure, the unremarkable evening that awaits Dorigen's small court. With equal

---

moot must   *sleep* slept   *Pernaso* Parnassus   *Scithero* Cicero   *orisonte* horizon   *reft* robbed   *solas* pleasure   *wrecche* miserable

---

fidelity to the narrator's characterisation, Chaucer gi
to clarify the misery of the lovesick Aurelius. But tha
the Franklin's sympathy for the one who is going t
villain of his piece. What follows is the real achieve
inadequacy with which Chaucer has endowed his n

> He to his hous is gon with sorweful herte.   (V

The contrast between 'hoom' and 'hous' is the co
group, secure in its ordinary purpose, and the soli
who is to break the pattern. The effect is intensifie
that follow, by the simple repetition of 'he' and 'h
narrator, for the moment, cannot take his eyes off th

> He seeth he may not fro his deeth asterte;
> Hym semed that he felte his herte colde.   (V

Aurelius's isolation from the others in the story is
narrator's sympathy reaches out to him. It is 'i
Franklin charitably insists, that Aurelius makes
Apollo:

> For verray wo out of his wit he breyde.
> He nyste what he spak, but thus he seyde . . .

And it is in his misery and literally in the darkness
more real by the Franklin's incapacity to dress up
Aurelius makes his 'pleynt'

> Unto the goddes, and first unto the *sonne*.   (V

A narrator who has his eye steadily on the acti
to the beginning of the episode. The sun's ecli
is ordinarily so natural as to be unremarkable. Bu
are about to meet one who, proposing to change
calls upon the sun to do his will.

---

asterte escape   *verray* excessive (cf. *verray feere*, line 860
Paradise itself, line 912)   *wit* mind   *breyde* went   *nyste*
didn't know

G

or, at a meeting between clerks,

> This Briton clerk hym asked of felawes
> The whiche that he had knowe in olde dawes.   (V 1179–80)

The Franklin's *forte* is certainly not set speech; but for brief phrase or plain silence he can hardly be equalled. Dorigen stands silent and incredulous at Aurelius's love-suit:

> He taketh his leve, and she astoned stood;
> In al hir face nas a drope of blood.
> She wende nevere han come in swich a trappe—   (V 1339–41)

and Chaucer has nothing to equal the single phrase the narrator puts into Arveragus's mouth as Dorigen ends her sad admission:

> This housbonde, with glad chiere, in freendly wyse
> Answerde and seyde as I shal yow devyse:
> '*Is ther oght elles, Dorigen, but this?*'   (V 1467–9)

In each of these last two instances Chaucer's technique is to allow the narrator's simplicity of statement to carry the essential weight of the story, as against the dutiful set-piece work that accompanies and contrasts with that simplicity. In the first example, the narrator's bleak comment 'She wende nevere han come in swich a trappe' precedes Dorigen's long 'compleynt'. The reality of the 'trap' is reinforced by something which is, again, acceptable primarily in terms of the Franklin's relative limitations as a narrator. Indeed, it is so acceptable that, very properly, it attracts no notice to itself. When Dorigen does speak, she repeats the run of the phrase which her narrator has already used—

> 'Allas,' quod she, 'that evere this sholde happe!
> For wende I nevere...'

We seem to hear the actress echoing what the author has set down for his character; and the effect is heightened by Dorigen standing, as it

---

felawes fellow-students, contemporaries   *dawes* days   *astoned* stunned
nas (= *ne* + *was*) was not   *wende* thought   *wyse* fashion   *oght* aught,
anything   *happe* happen   *wende* supposed, guessed

were, in the wings, ready to launch into her set speech, the long 'compleynt'. There could be no greater test of the audience's trust in a narrator. Dorigen's is a kind of shocked and therefore automatic response to her narrator's leading, comparable on its own level with Desdemona's 'Faith, half asleep'.[8]

If this exploits two distinctive characteristics of oral narration— unalterably serial presentation set against the peculiar limitations of any one narrator—Chaucer's skill is at once to move the speech into character. What is simply a trap to the Franklin, vigilant for his heroine, is to Dorigen a cruel prodigy, beyond all reason or natural expectation. She picks up her own lines—

> . . . wende I never by possibilitee
> That swich a monstre or merveille myghte be!
> It is agayns the proces of nature.   (V 1342–5)

The balance between narrator and character is restored; Dorigen is going her own way once more. But nothing could more potently give the sense of a near death-blow. The same principle, working this time almost exactly the other way around, is evident in the second instance, Dorigen's confession to Arveragus. She has, we are told, spoken at length; but the narrator spares us remorseless detail:

> 'Thus have I seyd,' quod she, 'thus have I sworn'—
> And toold hym al as ye han herd bifore;
> It nedeth nat reherce it yow namoore.   (V 1464–6)

This *occupatio*,[9] in its apparent clumsiness, even brutality, seals off the region of lament and explanation—and so brings into sharp focus the stillness of Arveragus who must wait to hear it all. Nothing could better bring out the newness of all this to Arveragus, its coming to him, as it cannot now come to the Franklin's audience, as entire shock.

In these and similar instances the Franklin's regard for his own audience parallels his compassion for the persons of his story—all of them, the naughty Aurelius not least; and this quality in him exemplifies the *gentillesse* which, firmly overriding Harry Bailly's objections, he

---

by possibilitee by (any) possibility (i.e. within the entire range of possibility)
monstre unnatural thing   *merveille* prodigy   *agayns* contrary to   *proces* course

sets himself to expound. All proceeds from a certain inadequacy in terms of literary art—which, at its worst, would be a sheer facility in discoursing on the point of honour (Harry Bailly's instinctive fear, perhaps). This obviously makes for humour; but it is also the foundation of our belief in the existence of the story and our trust—for as the story goes on we see there is no alternative—that the narrator will eventually pull it all into shape. Throughout we have the feeling, sometimes tantalising, sometimes nearly exasperating, that the story may evade the Franklin's best efforts—and best efforts they certainly are—to tell it.

The Franklin, then, steers his own unprofessional course, between knowledge of the story and what he chooses to give his audience. It is an attitude that, to take a leading instance, deliciously humanises the account of the magician's art, which sways between relish for all the jargon of the trade—

> his centris and his argumentz
> And his proporcioneles convenientz...
> Whan he hadde founde his firste mansioun,
> He knew the remenaunt by proporcioun...   (V 1277–8, 1285–6)

(all introduced, of course, under a disclaimer of knowledge of 'termes of astrologye'),[10] and on the other side, headshaking warnings to the audience that all this is very improper—

> swich a supersticious cursednesse—   (V 1272)

consisting, as it does, of

> swiche illusiouns and swiche meschaunces
> As hethen folk useden in thilke dayes   (V 1292–3)

It is between such quiet poles that all things in the story move. The harm that will threaten, like the magic art itself, is securely contained.

---

centris, argumentz means of determining the positions of planets
proporcioneles convenientz (lit.) fitting proportionals (tables for scaling down
general planetary motions)   *mansioun* position (of the moon)   *remenaunt*
rest (of the necessary data)   *proporcioun* proportionate calculation
supersticious supernatural   *cursednesse* wickedness, perversity   *meschaunces*
wicked practices

The narrator of *Troilus and Criseyde* was in an unhappily predestined position ('I, that God of Loves servantz serve'); but here a narrator who knows the end from the beginning himself constitutes a benevolent providence, steering his story to a happy ending.

How deeply is this interwoven in the fabric of the story? The morning which sees Aurelius and the magician on their way to Brittany to achieve their plan, was (the Franklin pauses, to give authoritative weight to this important date) 'as thise bokes me remembre'—

> The colde, frosty seson of Decembre.   (V 1244)

It is the time when all appearances are unpropitious:

> The bittre frostes, with the sleet and reyn,
> Destroyed hath the grene in every yerd.   (V 1250–1)

But in fact, and against these appearances, a rebirth of Nature is in prospect. It is Janus who stands at the gate of the year, and he looks both ways—suitably, for in Chaucer's working imagination January's bitter weather had paradoxically grown from a garden of perfected Spring (flowering in January in his source-story, *Il Filocolo*[11]). The story does its obvious work in the 'apparences' of magic, forecast by Aurelius's brother and fulfilled by the 'philosophre'. But Chaucer adds another dimension. From the mere contrast in his source between the summer and winter, to be changed by a trick, he leads to the real deception inherent in natural appearances. When the world is manifestly barren, it is in reality at its turning-point. With this changing of the seasons, another and greater promise lies in view. Chaucer's technique here is of great interest. As always, he works in and through his 'burel' narrator, who, predictably, begins with a rhetorical flight:

> Phebus wax old, and hewed lyk laton,
> That in his hoote declynacion
> Shoon as the burned gold with stremes brighte.   (V 1245–7)

---

yerd garden   *burel* homespun   *wax* grew   *hewed* coloured   *laton* copper
That (he) who   *his hoote declynacion* the celestial position (in relation to the Equator) where he gave most heat   *burned* burnished   *stremes* rays, beams

Admirable: but Phoebus, and the narrator with him, must come to the end of their trajectory—

> now in Capricorn adoun he lighte—

so we end with prosaic recognition:

> Wher as he shoon ful pale, *I dar wel seyn.*

No flights of fancy now. The monosyllables mark a return to unadorned reality. Outdoors there are 'The bittre frostes, with the sleet and reyn'; indoors, a very homely god sits by the fireside and celebrates Christmas:

> Janus sit by the fyr, with double berd,
> And drynketh of his bugle horn the wyn;
> Biforn hym stant brawen of the tusked swyn,
> And 'Nowel' crieth every lusty man.   (V 1252-5)

This prosaically comforting reminder is our assurance that whatever is to happen in apparent defiance of natural order can bring no final harm. The promise of a New Creation is placed on the margin of the Franklin's story. We are not to read into it an all-pervasive influence. But we are to see it, placed in this genial and unemphatic light, as not the least instance of an unobtrusively ordering imagination in the Franklin. This steadiness of aim, clearly (and most often humorously) distinguished from the wide-ranging knowledge and purposeful skills of a practised narrator, is rewarded by a full return of happiness. The artist who can in these terms defer to nature has nothing to learn of humility. Chaucer pays his tribute to innocence from a wealth of experience—in particular, a writer's experience of painfully recognising helpless suffering in his creatures. We were never to have, on any extended scale, the 'comedye' hoped for in the last twists and turns of *Troilus and Criseyde*. But the Franklin's Tale is the nearest to that fulfilment that can be imagined.

---

of his bugle horn from his drinking-horn (made from the horn of the wild ox) *stant* (stands) is set   *brawen* flesh   *lusty* jovial

(IV)

It is a tale which, whatever we may think of the existence of a 'Marriage Group', transcends the opposition between *auctoritee* and *experience* in the characterisation of the speaker no less than in the story he tells. There must be no striving for *maistrie*—above all in the practice of narrative art. Into the characterisation of the Franklin has gone all of Chaucer's own experience as a writer, taking his stand before a small and familiar audience and winning a measure of distance and hence comprehension by putting in play his own inadequacy. In so far as this is itself a courtesy towards his audience—a following-through, for the purposes of narration, of his actual relation to his courtly audience—it exemplifies the Franklin's *gentillesse*, a deference that is not amiable incomprehension, but remains shrewdly observant. Yet Chaucer's character may be said to improve upon his creator in two respects, both gained, we need not doubt, from hard-won experience. Chaucer's habitual standpoint of inadequacy was that of the clerk. What should *he* know of actuality? He must be obedient to what his 'olde bokes' tell him; and in the end he must abandon the story if he cannot bear to conclude it. The Franklin is under neither obligation. Disarmingly without pretence, he can only fall back on experience when deep matters and 'heigh style' prove too much for him. But this limitation means final freedom. He will persist in steering through to the happy ending he unashamedly wants for his creatures.

Chaucer is an artist who finds it difficult to bring things to an end. Does this perhaps reflect that 'tireless capacity' which Charles Muscatine finds in him 'for definition and comparison'?; or is it rather the inevitable outcome of 'a certain amiable inconsistency of tone, or of perspective, or of detail, as his narrative goes along'?[12] Both things are there. A criticism which concerns itself overmuch with tracking Chaucer down in what Lowes called his 'world of books' is perhaps preferable, if we have to choose between extremes, to one which labours to fit everything into a coherent design subtly achieved by Chaucer and there for our patient disentwining. But we shall do best if we relate both the zest for detail and the apparently free-wheeling inconsistency to that curiosity which the tales reflect and in their turn sustain. It is a curiosity which, on the writer's part, is stimulated by movement between the twin courts of appeal—*auctoritee* and *pref*. There is an ample scope and a perpetual stimulus for definition and comparison, a lively matching of individual detail with immovable archetypes; and, equally, for an amused eye, alert to mark discrepancy in behaviour or belief—most of all when the discrepancy remains wholly unsuspected by the subject, or the poet's own audience. So, on the one side, the attraction of inherent symmetry or correspondence, and their relations to final pattern; on the other, an unsleeping though never strident awareness of difference between what is and what is thought to be. But we must add to the account something derived from the same ultimate source—a sense of the writer's powerlessness, his inability to intervene, to shield his creatures from what must happen. Whether it comes 'of aventure or grace', the writer cannot *know*. In so far as his trade is in pre-existing story, there, in one sense, is an end of his responsibility. But it is at the same time the deepest root of his concern. That is an additional reason why, on the most serious occasions, he can, and even must, mix gravity and comedy. It is the least he can do if he is to deal honestly, reminding himself, as well as his audience, of the mere fluctuations of life:

Now up, now doun, as boket in a welle.

It is this unsleeping awareness—suspended only occasionally and then in favour of an entire simplicity—which makes Chaucer so markedly unlike all other writers in our tradition. Readers in many different generations may well be disappointed at this variability of tone and the uncertainties it produces in them. It is perhaps natural to think this quality a defect and ascribe it to the pioneering uncertainties of an early age, or, seizing upon it as a kind of authoritative ambivalence, to contend laboriously for its profound and many-sided significance in theological terms. Either way, and with whatever shades of intermediate reservation, the reader must reckon with an authorial incapacity for initiating and steadily fostering a single set of values in which the work is to be definitively understood. Whatever conclusion the present reader comes to, he will, I hope, place it to the

---

boket bucket

credit of Chaucer's account that this characteristic, so far from being
disabling, is the sufficient and lasting cause of his work moving, in
Raleigh's phrase 'the passion of curiosity'.[13] Chaucer's best effects
occur when the persons of his story, as some of his Dreamers and the
protagonists of his *tragedye*, appear to move beyond his control; or
when the narrators themselves, like the Franklin and most of the
Canterbury Pilgrims, were never wholly within it. On this condition
we have that sense of their free existence which is (to quote Raleigh
again) 'so entirely like life' as we encounter it that passionate curiosity
is renewed and rewarded at each successive reading.

Literary criticism, of course, can never be quite content with this
state of affairs; and with the frightening growth of purely pedagogical
interest in imaginative work the prospects of simple recognition become
more remote. Yet there are some signs that things may be changing.
That highly sophisticated criticism of the novel which could comfortably disparage the convention of an omniscient author has recently
been given some healthy knocks.[14] That may help us to reassess the
achievement of an author for whom a kind of accredited omniscience,
something inherent in the role of writer as dependant on the *auctoritees*,
can turn out to be uncrossable ignorance—and for that very reason can
allow no retreat into insentience. There is one obstacle removed.
Another may be going in the weakening of the long hold on criticism
of 'character-creation' as the supreme achievement of literary art. One
recent critic of the novel points out that in fact character-creation is
found more often today in inferior than in distinguished work, 'just
as accurate and vivacious representations of the human form are found
more often today in commercial rather than in original and imaginative
painting'. The 'characters' placed in review-order in the General
Prologue are, as we have seen, not always easily related to those set in
motion in end-link, prologue and tale: the achievement of *The
Canterbury Tales* remains. The critic I have quoted goes on: 'accuracy
is not enough. To convince us a character must also in a sense *surprise*
us, as a good poem or picture does'.[15] The character has a maximum
chance of doing that when it has come as a surprise to the writer himself—whether instantly recognised and faithfully responded to, or
slowly achieving distinctive stature as what was thought to be well-
founded knowledge begins to crumble. Either way, the reader's

continuing curiosity is the writer's achievement—a curiosity which the critic, however great his temptations, must not stifle at birth or waylay in infancy in the interests of some pretendedly comprehensive or edifying reading.

NOTES

INTRODUCTION

1. cf. D. S. Brewer, introducing a recent collection of critical studies: 'The most important development in medieval literary studies recently has been . . . a sharpened literary sense of the language the poet actually uses' (*Chaucer and Chaucerians*, Ed. Brewer, London 1966, Foreword).

2. Dryden, Preface to *Sylvae* (*Essays*, Ed. Ker, I, 254).

3. Charles Muscatine, '*The Canterbury Tales:* style of the man and style of the work', in *Chaucer and Chaucerians*, p. 89.

4. Bertrand H. Bronson, *In Search of Chaucer*, Toronto 1960, pp. 22–4.

5. *The Allegory of Love*, Oxford 1936, p. 170.

6. James J. Murphy, 'A New Look at Chaucer and the Rhetoricians', *R.E.S.*, n.s. XV (1964), 20. See also the discussion of 'The Art of Poetry' in A. C. Spearing, *Criticism and Medieval Poetry*, London 1964, pp. 46–67; and the same writer on Chaucer's rhetoric in his contribution to *An Introduction to Chaucer*, Cambridge 1965, pp. 102–14.

7. See Spearing, *Criticism and Medieval Poetry*, pp. 68 ff. (where the art of preaching is treated in relation to *Piers Plowman*).

8. *Poetria Nova*, lines 224–5 (text from Faral, *Les Arts Poétiques du XIIe et du XIIIe Siècle*, Paris 1924). On some salient differences between the pre- and post-printing eras, see H. J. Chaytor, *From Script to Print*, Cambridge 1945.

9. See Ruth Crosby, 'Oral Delivery in the Middle Ages', *Speculum*, XI (1968), 88–110; and, on Chaucer in particular, Bertrand H. Bronson, 'Chaucer's Art in Relation to his Audience' (*Five Studies in Literature*, Berkeley 1940, pp. 1–53). The frontispiece to MS Cambridge Corpus Christi College 61 shows Chaucer reciting at court. For a colour reproduction, and an attempted identification of other persons, see Margaret Galway, 'The "Troilus" Frontispiece', *Modern Language Review*, XLIV (1949), 161–77.

10. 'The Myth of Courtly Love', *Ventures* (Magazine of the Yale Graduate School), V (1965), no. 2, 16–23. More detailed reservations, in certain areas treated in C. S. Lewis's *Allegory of Love*, are made by contributors to *Patterns of Love and Courtesy: Essays in memory of C. S. Lewis*, edited by the present writer, London 1966.

11. Ian Bishop, reviewing (in *Medium Ævum*, XXXII (1963), 238–42) Bernard F. Huppé and D. W. Robertson, Jr., *Fruyt and Chaf: Studies in Chaucer's Allegories*, Princeton 1963. A full-scale statement of aims and working principles is to be found in D. W. Robertson's *A Preface to Chaucer*, Princeton 1963. (Among reviews, that by Francis Lee Utley, 'Robertsonianism Redivivus', *Romance Philology*, XIX (1965), 250–60, should not be missed.)

12. Bernard F. Huppé, *A Reading of the Canterbury Tales*, New York 1964, pp. 236–7.

13. Muscatine, in *Chaucer and Chaucerians*, pp. 89, 93.

14. *The Discarded Image: an introduction to medieval and renaissance literature*, Cambridge 1964.

15. The remark is Ruskin's. See Kathleen Tillotson, 'The Tale and the Teller' (London 1959), for an application to Dickens.

CHAPTER I

1. See the colour reproduction referred to above, note 9 of Introduction. Black and white reproductions are readily accessible—for example, the frontispiece to *Chaucer's Major Poetry*, Ed. Albert C. Baugh, New York 1963.

2. I keep the familiar modernised titles. But it should be observed that 'hous' has a rather more scientific flavour than 'house'; 'fame' is much nearer the sense 'speech', 'utterance' than the abstract quality 'reputation' (indeed, the whole point of the journey undertaken in Book II is the attempt to track down sound waves); and a 'Parliament of Fowls' must not be allowed to suggest Westminster in the Barnyard, but simply an 'Assembly of Birds'.

3. 'The Pattern of Consolation in *The Book of the Duchess*', *Speculum*, XXXI (1956), 626–48 (reprinted in *Chaucer Criticism*, vol. II (*Troilus and Criseyde and the Minor Poems*) Ed. Schoeck and Taylor, Notre Dame 1961, pp. 232–60).

4. See below, Chapter 4.

5. It is worth pointing out that on appointment as Controller in the Port of London Chaucer was formally required to keep the books in his 'very own hand'. No deputising whatever was to be countenanced. (*Ita quod idem Galfridus rotulos suos dicta officia tangentes manu sua propria scribat et continue moretur ibidem et omnia que ad officia illa pertinent in propria persona sua et non per substitutum suum faciat et exequatur: Chaucer Life-Records*, Ed. Crow and Olson, Oxford 1966, p. 148.)

6. The most influential example is Boethius, *Consolation of Philosophy*, where

the 'I' of the story is soundly taken to task by Philosophy. She has no patience with her self-absorbed pupil: '*Sentisne,*' inquit, '*haec atque animo inlabuntur tuo, an ὄνος λύρας? Quid fles, quid lacrimis manas?*

᾿Εξαύδα, μὴ κεῦθε νόῳ.

Si operam medicantis exspectas, oportet uulnus detegas.' 'Felistow', quod sche, 'thise thynges, and entren thei aught in thy corage? Artow like an asse to the harpe? Why wepistow, why spillestow teeris? Yif thou abidest after help of thi leche, the byhoveth discovre thy wownde' (Book I, pr. 4; Chaucer does not translate the quotation from Homer—'Speak out; don't keep hidden in your mind . . .')

7. For a convenient summary of the devices of 'rhetoric' see the Appendix to J. W. H. Atkins, *English Literary Criticism: The Medieval Phase*, Cambridge 1943 (pp. 200–3).

8. The *Oraculum* is that kind of dream in which a venerable person appears, to announce a solemn truth. The common classification of dreams was in terms of the psychological faculty from which they were thought to derive. Significant dreams—those which were veridical in content—came from the Reason; and besides the *Oraculum* there were the *Visio* (direct prevision of the future) and the *Somnium* (a dream which disguised its purport under type and symbol and therefore needed skilled interpretation). From the Fancy came non-significant dream-experience—the *Insomnium* (or non-dream), a mechanical repetition of dominant interest or preoccupation; and the *Visum* (also called the *Phantasma*), something seen between waking and sleeping—perhaps like Alice's experience in crossing the frontier from the dream of wonderland to waking consciousness, when the noise of the Court proceedings begins to merge with packing up the picnic basket. Macrobius is the revered exponent of this system. See also, below, n. 22 of Chapter 5.

9. On 'Natura, Nature, and Kind' see the Appendix to J. A. W. Bennett, *The Parlement of Foules*, Oxford 1957, pp. 194–212.

10. *Letters of John Keats*, Ed. Maurice Buxton Forman, 3rd edn., Oxford 1947, p. 67 (letter to Benjamin Bailey, 22 November 1817).

11. Thomas Hardy, *The Life and Death of the Mayor of Casterbridge*, conclusion.

12. See R. G. Collingwood, *The Principles of Art*, Oxford 1938, ch. IV, in particular pp. 69–77.

---

corage heart, mind   *abidest after* look for, expect   *leche* physician   *the*
byhoveth you must   *discovre* disclose

CHAPTER 2

1. A. C. Baugh (Ed.), *Chaucer's Major Poetry* (New York 1963), p. 81.

2. Robert A. Pratt ('Chaucer and *Le Roman de Troyle et de Criseida*', *Studies in Philology*, LIII (1956), 509–39) shows that in a number of details (including some 'which seem to make the story or the characters more gentle, noble, or courteous') the *Roman* is closer to Chaucer's work than is *Il Filostrato*. It seems reasonable to accept the hypothesis that Chaucer 'as he wrote . . . had before him both *Il Filostrato* and *Le Roman de Troyle*'. The matter is, however, one of verbal detail. The major changes in theme and standpoint set out in C. S. Lewis's 'What Chaucer really did to *Il Filostrato*' (*Essays and Studies*, XVII (1932), 56–75, reprinted in Schoeck and Taylor, *Chaucer Criticism: Troilus and Criseyde and the Minor Poems*, pp. 16–33) are substantially unaffected. For a detailed comparison of Chaucer's poem with the relevant parts of *Il Filostrato* (translated), see W. M. Rossetti's edition for the Chaucer Society (1873).

3. See Charles A. Owen ('The significance of Chaucer's revisions of *Troilus and Criseyde*', *Modern Philology*, LV (1957), 1–5).

4. (Ed.) *Chaucer's Poetry* (New York 1958), p. 966.

5. Pandarus is cheerfully disingenuous. In its plainer form the proverb runs

> unto shrewes joye it is and ese
> To have hir felawes in peyne and disese.   (*C.T.* VIII, 746–7)

6. An opposition which Chaucer sharpens, from

> E già veduto s'è andare il losco
> Dove l'illuminato *non va bene*.   (*Il Fil.* ii, 10)

to —

> I have myself ek seyn a blynd man goo
> Ther as *he fel* that couthe loken wide.

7.
> le genti dolorose,
> ch'hanno perduto il ben dello intelletto.   (*Inferno* iii, 17–18)

8. *Piers Plowman* B V, 238–9.

9. *Il Filostrato* ii, 54. Chaucer remodels the passage to make it apply to both lovers:

> Thenk ek how elde wasteth every houre
> In eche of yow a partie of beautee;
> And *therefore* . . .   (II, 393–5)

10.
> i' non son cruda
> Come ti par, nè sì di pietà nuda . . .
>
> Ma per fuggir vergogna, e forse peggio,
> Pregalo che sia saggio, e faccia quello
> Che a me biasmo non sia, nè anche ad ello.   (ii, 65–6)

---

shrewes rascals   *disese* trouble   *goo* walk (upright)   *elde* age

11. cf. 'Fulfyld of thought and busy hevynesse', *PF* 89. The image of 'bisi-nesse' uppermost in Criseyde's mind may be Pandarus, confessing how he wormed out Troilus's secret—

> God woot, nevere, sith that I was born,
> Was I so *besy* no man for to preche—   (568–9)

where Chaucer is rendering 'con nuova arte e con diverso ingegno' (ii, 63).

12.   un troian giovinetto,
> D'alto lignaggio e molto coraggioso.   (ii, 1)

He had earlier claimed to have experienced 'that wretched fire':

> Io provai già per la mia gran follia
> Qual fosse questo maladetto fuoco.

So he can appropriately deride Pandaro's claim to satisfy *him* in the present instance:

>   Come avuto
> Da te l'avrei, che sempre te doglioso
> Per amor vidi, e non ten sai atare?
> Me dunque come credi sodisfare?   (ibid., 9)

13. *Il Filostrato* ii, 23–7.

14. 'Distance and Predestination in *Troilus and Criseyde*', *PMLA*, LXXII (1957), 14–26 (reprinted in Schoeck and Taylor, *Chaucer Criticism: Troilus and Criseyde and the Minor Poems*, pp. 196–210, to which subsequent reference is made).

15. Schoeck and Taylor, p. 204.

16. E. T. Donaldson, 'The ending of Chaucer's *Troilus*', *Early English and Norse Studies presented to Hugh Smith*, Ed. A. Brown and P. Foote (London 1963), p. 37.

17. '*Troilus and Criseyde*: a reconsideration', in *Patterns of Love and Courtesy: Essays in memory of C. S. Lewis*, p. 105.

18. *The Allegory of Love*, p. 195.

19. 'Second Thoughts: C. S. Lewis on Chaucer's *Troilus*', *Essays in Criticism*, VIII (1958), 127.

20. cf. 'There were some cheerless aspects about the usually pleasant work of construction. There was poor Maria; here she was on her honeymoon, entering into married life, having children. I knew the fate in store for her, and the fate in store for those children ... there was little that I could do for her. At least I saved her from disillusionment; I could help her in a negative kind of way, but I could not allow sentiment to spoil the story' (C. S. Forester, *The Hornblower Companion* (London 1964), p. 131).

21. *Journals*, 11 September 1931. Quoted in Miriam Allott, *Novelists on the Novel* (London 1959), p. 290.

CHAPTER 3

1. *Inferno*, vii, 81.

2. *Consolation of Philosophy*, V, vi.

3. *The Allegory of Love*, p. 195.

4. See p. 43–4, 57 above.

5. Walter Raleigh, *Milton*, London 1900, p. 141.

6. Letter to Mme Roger Des Genettes (October–November 1856): *Correspondance*, Paris 1927, IV, 134.

7. D. H. Lawrence, *Studies in Classic American Literature*, Phoenix edition, London 1964, p. 2.

8. 'Second Thoughts: C. S. Lewis on Chaucer's *Troilus*', 128.

CHAPTER 4

1. Quotations from the Prologue, unless otherwise noted, are from the F version, which from the evidence of the manuscripts would seem to be the earlier version. (The fact that G, the later version, is in many respects inferior, is no argument against Chaucer's authorship of it. Writers do not invariably improve their work on revision.)

2. Modern readers may best be introduced to the distinction between 'kan' and 'knowen' by two successive stanzas of the Man of Law, a careful speaker. In the first, he emphasises that God's ways lie beyond even learned understanding—we

> for oure ignorance
> Ne *konne* noght knowe his prudent purveiance;

but he goes on to stress that God's works are manifest to the simplest of men:

> Wel *may* men knowe it was no wight but he . . . (II, 483, 488)

A more moving contrast occurs in Book V of *Troilus and Criseyde*. Waiting on the walls of Troy, Troilus and Pandarus see Criseyde in every incoming figure—

> every maner wight
> That com fro fer, they seyden it was she,
> Til that thei *koude* knowen hym aright—

that is, until they were able to make out who in fact it was. On the other hand, grief so undoes Troilus that he almost loses the semblance of humanity:

> He so defet was, that no manere man
> Unneth hym *myghte* knowen ther he wente— (V, 1115–17; 1219–20)

No question of special knowledge, now. Hardly anyone could tell that it was Troilus.

3. See below, p. 104.

4. The *Roman de la Rose* is the most remarkable of those medieval works which, celebrating an ideal, have to admit its actual rarity. The *Roman* is the work of two authors—Guillaume de Lorris and Jean de Meun, his continuator. The God of Love is, clearly, thinking of the antifeminist satire of Jean de Meun, and (characteristically) equating it with the whole content of the *Roman*. (For an exposition of the *Roman*, see C. S. Lewis, *The Allegory of Love*, pp. 112–56; and Charles Muscatine, *Chaucer and the French Tradition*, Berkeley and Los Angeles 1957, pp. 30–41, 71–97.)

5. cf. below, p. 149–50.

6. The other candidate is Valerius Maximus, author of *De factis dictisque memorabilibus*, whom the Wife of Bath had had cause to note (III, 460–3, 643–58). (Robert Pratt points out that most medieval readers attributed the *Epistola* to him: 'Chaucer and the hand that fed him', *Speculum*, XLI (1966), 638, n. 56.) The point of my argument is unaffected by precise identification of 'Valerye'.

7. See Howard Schless, 'Chaucer and Dante', in *Critical Approaches to Medieval Literature*, Selected Papers from the English Institute, New York 1958–9, pp. 141–5.

8. Robinson, p. 482.

CHAPTER 5

1. *Some Authors*, Oxford 1923, p. 5.

2. Preface to *The Fables* (*Essays of John Dryden*, Ed. Ker, Oxford 1926, II, 262).

3. cf. D. S. Brewer, 'Images of Chaucer, 1386–1900', in *Chaucer and Chaucerians*, p. 253. The quotation is from Peter Betham (1544).

4. *The Allegory of Love*, p. 162.

5. Austin, Texas 1955. Mr Lumiansky adroitly moves in one sentence from harmless assumption to critical certainty: 'The indisputable point here seems to be that Chaucer not only came in contact with human beings of all sorts in the course of his long public career as diplomat and civil servant, but that he took full advantage of the opportunity to observe closely the features, dress, habits, manners, quirks, affectations, and eccentricities of the people he met; *and then, because of his interest in, and his keen observation of, mankind, he regularly conceived and developed his narratives as vehicles for character portrayal*' (p. 3: italics supplied). Short work! Mr Lumiansky ostensibly devotes ten pages (pp. 3–12) to what he calls 'The point of view and the assumptions'. But the point of view is so flexible as to include Kemp Malone's flat denial of any 'dramatic approach' (p. 5); and the assumptions are wholly governed by the conviction that 'the Pilgrims and their stories exist for the sake of themselves and, at the same time, for the sake of each other' (p. 7): so there is no impediment to thorough-going drama. The General Prologue and the links are 'The Movable Stage'; and we can settle down to enjoy, or endure, 'The Twenty-three Performances'.

6. 'Chaucer's Art in Relation to his Audience' (in *Five Studies in Literature*), p. 53.

7. The most notable is the description of Custance as she stands before her accusers:

> Have ye nat seyn somtyme a pale face
> Among a prees, of hym that hath be lad
> Toward his deeth . . . ?   (II, 645 ff.)

8. cf. Lumiansky who says (p. 71), somewhat dispiritedly, '. . . one can maintain—successfully, I think—that the story and its teller *are not completely unsuited*' (italics supplied).

9. G. H. Gerould has the pleasing suggestion that 'this alestake' where the Pardoner pauses is in fact the Pardoner's bosom companion, the Summoner—with the garland perched on his head 'As greet as it were for an ale-stake' (I, 667), and a 'cake' (carried as a 'bokeleer') all ready to hand (*Chaucerian Essays*, Princeton 1952, pp. 55–8). If so, the Pardoner's flair for improvisation is already apparent. A narrator who can turn his confederate into a wayside inn is one who can at the right time shape his fellow-Pilgrims into a rapt congregation.

10. *Biographia Literaria*, ch. XIII.

11. cf. He 'has not always been an assassin of souls. He is a renegade, perhaps, from some holy order' (*Chaucer and his poetry*, Cambridge, Mass. 1915, pp. 216–17).

12. *Piers Plowman*, A, II, 183–4 (Kane).

13. E. T. Donaldson, 'Idiom of Popular Poetry in the *Miller's Tale*', *English Institute Essays*, 1950 (New York 1951), pp. 116–40.

14. J. R. R. Tolkien, 'Chaucer as a philologist: *The Reeve's Tale*', *Philological Society's Transactions*, 1934, 1–70; 3.

15. It may be convenient at this point to remind the reader that of the thirty-two Pilgrims who could be expected to tell a tale (excluding the Host, as master of ceremonies) only twenty-three are called into action (and only Chaucer himself tells a second tale, though this 'second' tale is really a substitution for a bad first shot). As matters stand, we do not have these twenty-four tales arranged in a coherent sequence, but instead there are ten separate divisions (sometimes called 'fragments', though the word is possibly misleading, since one of the divisions—that which includes Chaucer's and the Monk's tales—is a fully articulated series of six tales). The order in the manuscripts does not notably help; however highly modern readers may rate the realism of the enveloping narrative, one medieval grouping places tales told near Canterbury among the earlier ones. Alternative arrangements have of course been proposed. But in the absence of any definitive arrangement by the author, it is as well to accept the order which has good manuscript authority and is followed in most modern editions, including Robinson.

16. E. T. Donaldson, 'Chaucer the Pilgrim' (in Schoeck and Taylor, *Chaucer Criticism: The Canterbury Tales*, p. 5).

17. Nevill Coghill, *The Poet Chaucer*, London 1967, p. 117.

18. For possible satire on contemporary Flemish knighthood, see J. M. Manly, 'Sir Thopas: a satire', in *Essays and Studies*, XIII (1928), 52–73.

19. Siegfried Sassoon, *Memoirs of a Fox-Hunting Man*, London 1937, Part Nine: 'In the Army'.

20. A. C. Spearing, 'Chaucer the Writer', in *An Introduction to Chaucer*, pp. 148–9.

21. The document is given in *Chaucer Life-Records*, Ed. Crow and Olson, pp. 91–3.

22. For a convenient account of the Macrobian classification of dreams, see W. C. Curry, *Chaucer and the Medieval Sciences*, 2nd edn., New York 1960, pp. 199–202.

23. In his 'opposition' paper, 'Patristic Exegesis in the Criticism of Medieval Literature' (*Critical Approaches to Medieval Literature*, pp. 1–26).

24. *Gentillesse* is the high conduct that might be looked for in the *gentil*, those of good birth. Like other ideals, it is prized for its rarity. But, as the Franklin goes on to demonstrate, a clerk and a squire, given the right lead, can behave as 'gentilly' as any knight. Example is all.

25. The Wife of Bath had worked towards a sufficient definition of *gentillesse*: 'he is gentil that dooth gentil dedis' (III, 1170; see also 113–16 and 1129–30). As Phyllis Hodgson observes in her model edition of the Franklin's Tale (London 1960), Alice's 'church-going and her scholar-husband's reading had left some impression upon her'. Perhaps we might credit all her deceased husbands with a share in her education. Learned and 'lewed' alike, they deserve a clerkly epitaph: *pereunt nec imputantur*.

26. G. H. Gerould chivalrously hastened to defend the Franklin against Root's charge that 'he can never be quite the complete gentleman', but succeeded only in showing that the position of a franklin was highly variable, and that the 'individual characteristics and distinctions' which Chaucer gives his Franklin 'throw light on the possibilities open to his rank' ('The Social Status of the Franklin', *Chaucerian Essays*, p. 43).

27. Lumiansky, p. 249.

CHAPTER 6

1. Robinson, p. 7. Kittredge's original article, 'Chaucer's discussion of marriage', is reprinted in Schoeck and Taylor, vol. I (pp. 130–59), with references to subsequent discussion.

2. Phyllis Hodgson (Ed.), *The Franklin's Tale*, p. 31.

3. ibid., p. 14.

4. I except, of course, those professional readers whose critical principles require that every work of imagination should have a discoverable, if recondite, meaning and every question therefore an authoritative answer. Mr Bernard Huppé, for example, is in no doubt and finds for the clerk—who (perhaps in this resembling Mr Huppé himself) 'has taken on a task of great difficulty, not out of need, but in order to be obliging' (*A Reading of the Canterbury Tales*, Albany, N.Y. 1964, p. 174).

5. 'The Autobiographical Fallacy in Chaucer and Langland Studies', Chambers Memorial Lecture, London 1965, p. 15.

6. *The Allegory of Love*, p. 170. He is followed, for example, by D. S. Brewer (*Chaucer*, London 1953, p. 47).

7. The serious imitation of this in the *Kingis Quair*, st. 72, is, of course, no limitation upon our assessing Chaucer's humorous use of high and low language—any more than Ellesmere's singling out Dorigen's 'compleynt' as a virtuoso performance—*The compleynt of Dorigene ayeyns Fortune*—must silence all comment in face of an approved star turn. The author of the *Kingis Quair*, since he is dealing in fine writing not dramatic speech, understandably tries to go one better than Chaucer. After the descent from high to low—

> The long day thus gan I prye and pour,
> Till Phebus endit had his bemes bryght,
> And bad go farewele every lef and flour,
> This is to say, approch gan the nyght—

up he goes once more—

> And Esperus his lampis gan to light.

Chaucer's neat bathos is replaced by a sort of aureate sandwich.

8. *Othello* iv, 2, 99 (New Arden).

9. The 'refusal to describe' is a device which suits Chaucer very well, enabling him, most often, to close the range between himself and the audience. For an attractive account of nine instances of 'amplification' see the edition of the Nun's Priest's Tale by Nevill Coghill and Christopher Tolkien (London 1959), pp. 46–50. (Categorisations of systematic 'rhetoric' are given in E. Faral, *Les Arts Poétiques du XIIe et du XIIIe Siècle*; J. W. H. Atkins, *English Literary Criticism: the Medieval Phase*; etc. But wholesale application to Chaucer should, as is suggested in the Introduction to this book, be treated with reserve.)

10. On the Franklin's terminology, see Appendix IV of Phyllis Hodgson's edition of the Tale.

11. For text, see Bryan and Dempster, *Sources and Analogues of Chaucer's Canterbury Tales*, Chicago 1940, pp. 377–83. The tale is taken from the episode of the 'Questions', thirteen in all. 'H.G.''s agreeable sixteenth-century rendering has been reprinted in *Thirteen Questions of Love*, London 1927. The story is summarised in Phyllis Hodgson's edition of the Tale (pp. 15–18).

12. *Chaucer and the French Tradition*, p. 223; 'The Canterbury Tales: style of the man and style of the work', in *Chaucer and Chaucerians*, p. 89.

13. See above, p. 105.

14. See Wayne C. Booth, *The Rhetoric of Fiction*, Chicago 1961. The elimina-·
tion of the omniscient author in favour of the pretendedly superior mode of
indirect narration overlooks the implied author or 'second self', present in all
successful narrative art; and the real distinction is shown to be between 'reliable'
and 'unreliable' narrators. See also W. J. Harvey, *Character and the Novel*,
London 1965, especially ch. IV, 'Character and Narration', pp. 74–99.

15. John Bayley, reviewing *Character and the Novel*, in *Review of English
Studies*, n.s. XVII (1966), 453.

SELECTED BIBLIOGRAPHY

1. BIBLIOGRAPHICAL

Hammond, E. P., *Chaucer: A Bibliographical Manual*, New York 1908

Griffith, D. D., *Bibliography of Chaucer, 1908–1953*, Seattle 1955

2. BIOGRAPHICAL, AND BACKGROUND STUDIES

Brewer, Derek, *Chaucer in his time*, London 1963

Bronson, B. H., 'Chaucer's art in relation to his audience', in *Five Studies in Literature*, Berkeley 1940

Chaucer Life-Records, Ed. M. M. Crow and C. C. Olson, Oxford 1966

Chaytor, H. J., *From Script to Print*, Cambridge 1945

Curry, W. C., *Chaucer and the Mediaeval Sciences*, 2nd edn., New York 1960

Lewis, C. S., *The Allegory of Love*, Oxford 1936

Loomis, R. S., *A Mirror of Chaucer's World*, Princeton 1965

McKisack, M., *The Fourteenth Century, 1307–1399*, Oxford 1959

Rickert, Edith (compiler), *Chaucer's World*, Ed. C. C. Olson and M. M. Crow, New York 1948

Robertson, D. W., *A Preface to Chaucer*, Princeton 1962

3. EDITIONS

The Complete Works of Geoffrey Chaucer, Ed. W. W. Skeat, 7 vols., Oxford 1894–7. (Oxford Chaucer)

The Works of Geoffrey Chaucer, Ed. F. N. Robinson, 2nd edn., Boston 1957. (New Cambridge Edition)

Chaucer's Poetry: an anthology for the modern reader, Ed. E. T. Donaldson, New York 1958

Chaucer's Major Poetry, Ed. A. C. Baugh, New York 1963

(Translation) Coghill, Nevill, *Geoffrey Chaucer: The Canterbury Tales translated into modern English*, London 1952

4. INTERPRETATION AND CRITICISM

Bennett, H. S., *Chaucer and the Fifteenth Century*, Oxford 1947

Brewer, D. S., *Chaucer*, London 1953

Brewer, D. S. (Ed.), *Chaucer and Chaucerians*, London 1966

Bronson, B. H., *In Search of Chaucer*, Toronto 1957

Clemen, Wolfgang, *Chaucer's Early Poetry*, London 1963

Coghill, N., *The Poet Chaucer*, 2nd. edn., London 1967

Gerould, G. H., *Chaucerian Essays*, Princeton 1952

Huppé, B. F., *A Reading of the Canterbury Tales*, Albany, N.Y. 1964

Hussey, Maurice, with A. C. Spearing and James Winny, *An Introduction to Chaucer*, Cambridge 1965

Kittredge, G. L., *Chaucer and His Poetry*, Cambridge, Mass. 1915

Lawrence, W. W., *Chaucer and the Canterbury Tales*, New York 1950

Lowes, J. L., *Geoffrey Chaucer*, Oxford 1934

Lumiansky, R. M., *Of Sondry Folk: The Dramatic Principle in the Canterbury Tales*, Austin, Texas 1955

Malone, K., *Chapters on Chaucer*, Baltimore 1951

Manly, J. M., *Some New Light on Chaucer*, New York 1926

Muscatine, C., *Chaucer and the French Tradition: A Study in Style and Meaning*, Berkeley and Los Angeles 1957

Patch, H. E., *On Rereading Chaucer*, Cambridge, Mass. 1939

Root, R. K., *The Poetry of Chaucer*, 2nd edn., Boston 1922

Tatlock, J. S. P., *The Mind and Art of Chaucer*, Syracuse 1950

For useful reprinting of major essays, see

Chaucer Criticism, Ed. R. Schoeck and J. Taylor (vol. I, *The Canterbury Tales*; vol. II, *Troilus and Criseyde and the Minor Poems*), Indiana 1961, 1962 (Notre Dame Books)

Chaucer: modern essays in criticism, Ed. E. Wagenknecht, New York 1959 (Galaxy Books)

Discussions of the Canterbury Tales, Ed. C. A. Owen, Boston 1961 (Discussions of Literature)

INDEX

AFRICANUS, SCIPIO, 36–7
Allott, Miriam, 169
Anne of Bohemia, 104
Atkins, J. W. H., 167, 174
'augmentation', 11
'aureate' language, 129–30, 174

BAUGH, A. C., 47, 166
Bayley, John, 162
Bennett, Arnold, 68–9
Bennett, J. A. W., 167
Beryn, Tale of, 106
Betham, Peter, 106
Bishop, Ian, 17
Blanche, Duchess of Lancaster, 19, 66
Bloomfield, M. W., 55, 63–4
Boccaccio, 47 ff., 94, 105, 158, 168–9, 174
Boethius, 39, 71–2, 147, 166–7
Booth, Wayne C., 175
Bovary, Emma, 87–8
Bradley, A. C., 17
Brewer, D. S., 165, 171, 174
Bronson, Bertrand H., 12, 108, 165
Bryan, W. F. (with G. Dempster), 174

CAPELLA, MARTIANUS, 39

Chaytor, H. J., 165
Chesterton, G. K., 136
Coghill, Nevill, 105, 124, 174
Coleridge, S. T., 113
Collingwood, R. G., 167
Confessio Amantis, see Gower, John
Corpus Christi College MS, 19–20, 165, 166
'Courtly Love', 16–17, 166
Crosby, Ruth, 165
Crow, M. M. (with C. C. Olson), 166, 173
Curry, W. C., 173

DAISY, cult of, 99, 104
Dante, 30, 50, 70
de Contemptu Mundi, 109
de Gaultier, Jules, 88
de Planctu Naturae, 39
demande, 147
Dickens, Charles, 166
Donaldson, E. T., 16, 48–9, 64, 117, 124, 133
Dryden, John, 11, 105–6, 107, 139
Dumas, Alexandre, 68
Dunbar, William, 106

ELIOT, T. S., 68

Ellesmere MS, 174
exclamatio, 31
exemplum, 123, 149

fabliau, 13, 116, 118, 123, 138
Faral, E., 165, 174
Flaubert, Gustave, 87–9
Forester, C. S., 169
Friendly animal (convention), 28–30

GALWAY, MARGARET, 165
gentillesse, 143, 145, 151, 156, 160, 173
Gerould, G. H., 172, 173
Gower, John, 106–7

HARDY, THOMAS, 46, 73
Harvey, W. J., 175
Henryson, Robert, 89
Hoccleve, Thomas, 106
Hodgson, Phyllis, 145–6, 173, 174
Hugh of Lincoln, 131
Huppé, Bernard F., 17, 166, 174
Huxley, Aldous, 130

insomnium, 132, 167

JEROME ('agayns Jovynyan'), 100
John of Gaunt, 19, 21, 26

KANE, GEORGE, 147
Keats, John, 45, 76
Kingis Quair, 174
Kittredge, G. L., 113, 140, 173

LANGLAND, WILLIAM, 50, 113, 165
Lawlor, John, 26, 166

Lawrence, D. H., 88
Lewis, C. S., 12, 18, 47, 49, 66, 73,
    106, 147, 166, 168, 171
Lowes, J. L., 130, 160
Lumiansky, R. M., 108, 137, 172
Lydgate, John, 106

MACHAUT, GUILLAUME DE, 26, 30
Macrobius, 37, 167, 173; *see also*
    insomnium, *oraculum*
Malone, Kemp, 171
Manly, J. M., 173
Mansfield, 2nd Lieut., 129
Map, Walter, 100
Murphy, James J., 14
Muscatine, Charles, 12, 17–18, 160,
    171

occupatio, 31, 81, 94, 156, 174
Olson, C. C. (with M. M. Crow),
    166, 173
oraculum, 36, 167
Othello, 156
Ovid, 13, 100
Owen, Charles A., 48, 168

PHILIPPA (Chaucer), 131
Piers Plowman, see Langland, William
Poetria Nova, 15
Pratt, Robert A., 168, 171

RALEIGH, WALTER, 82, 105, 162
Rhetoric, 14–15, 134, 152, 158, 165,
    167, 174; *see also occupatio*,
    exemplum, etc.
Robertson, D. W., 17, 166
Robinson, F. N., 10, 104, 140, 172
Romance of the Rose, 13, 99, 171

Root, R. K., 173
Rossetti, W. M., 168
Ruskin, John, 18

SALTER, ELIZABETH, 64
Samson Agonistes, 73
Sassoon, Siegfried, 173
Schless, Howard, 171
Sharrock, Roger, 68, 89
Spearing, A. C., 14, 130–1
Speculum Historiale, 100

Spenser, Edmund, 11, 106

THACKERAY, W. M., 35
Tillotson, Kathleen, 166
Tolkien, Christopher, 174
Tolkien, J. R. R., 117

UTLEY, F. L., 166

'VALERYE', 100, 171